DELOG

DELOG

JOURNEY TO REALMS
BEYOND DEATH

Delog Dawa Drolma

*Translated from the Tibetan by
Richard Barron under the direction of
His Eminence Chagdud Tulku Rinpoche*

Padma Publishing

Published by Padma Publishing
P.O. Box 279
Junction City, CA 96048

Printed in the United States of America

99 98 97 96   5 4 3 2

Cover by Carol Skylark

Library of Congress Cataloging-in-Publication Data

Delog Dawa Drolma
Delog: journey to realms beyond death / Delog Dawa Drolma; translated
by Richard Barron.

p. cm.

ISBN 1-881847-05-5

1. Intermediate state—Buddhism. 2. Eschatology, Buddhist.
3. Near-death experience—Religious aspects—Buddhism. I. Barron,
Richard. II. Title
BQ4490.D37 1995
294.3'423—dc20   94-22389
                                                            CIP

ISBN 1-881847-05-5 Paperback

CONTENTS

INTRODUCTION

CHAGDUD TULKU

༄༅། As a child in Tibet, I sometimes found my mother, Delog Dawa Drolma, surrounded by an audience listening with utmost attention as she told of her journeys to other realms. Her face was radiant as she spoke of the deities in the pure realms; tears flowed as she described the miseries of hell beings and *pretas*, or tormented spirits. She told of encountering deceased relatives of certain people, and she relayed from the dead to the living concerns about unfinished business (perhaps buried coins or jewels that could not be located) or pleas for prayers and ceremonies. She also brought back spiritual advice from high lamas who had passed from this world, to which lamas on this side of death responded with deep respect.

My mother was revered throughout Tibet for her extraordinary powers as a lama, but she was more famous for being a *delog* (pronounced *DAY-loak*), one who has crossed the threshold of death and returned to tell about it. Hers was not a visionary or momentary near-death experience. For five full days she lay cold, breathless, and devoid of any vital signs, while her consciousness moved freely into other realms, often escorted by the wisdom goddess White Tara. She undertook her journey as a delog according to instructions she had received from Tara in visions, but against the wishes of her lamas, who pleaded with her not to take such a risk.

It is remarkable that she, a young woman of sixteen, had so much confidence in her meditation that she prevailed over very wise, much older lamas. However, she herself had been recognized as an emanation of White Tara, a powerful force of enlightened mind for the longevity and liberation of sentient beings. Throughout her childhood Dawa Drolma showed a remarkable depth of compassion. No beggar who came to our tent left without her offering whatever she could put her hands on—my family took to hiding its valuables lest she give them away.

Our family's black felt tent could hold four hundred people during great ceremonies. Dawa Drolma was honored with a throne along with the other high lamas, including her four uncles, who were famous throughout eastern Tibet. She herself was a perfectionist in the performance of ritual. Several years ago I met a monk who remembered her wrath when he blew his *kangling* (ceremonial trumpet) poorly. Her presence inspired both care in the effortful steps of practice and recognition that the underlying nature of these steps is effortless awareness.

Her dreams and visions were revelations of realization, and those leading up to her delog experience were unmistakably clear in their instructions. The fears of the lamas who urged her not to undertake such a journey, but rather to fast, take medicine, and perform ceremonies, were not groundless, however—after she had died and gone to Padmasambhava's pure realm, she met her late uncle, the revered master Khakyod Wangpo, who warned her that it would be dangerous for her to remain and told her that she should return to the human realm to benefit beings.

Later, when she traveled through the *bardo*, or intermediate state between death and rebirth, and the hell and preta realms, an emanation of the feminine deity Vajravarahi expressed doubt that Dawa Drolma would be able to bring about much benefit. "It may be necessary for you, my girl, to return to the human realm. But . . . having taken rebirth as a woman, you will have little authority. . . . Sentient beings in these degenerate times will be hard put to believe that your accounts are true."

White Tara took issue with this statement, saying, "She is a heroine with a courageous mind," and adding that she had not listened to those who had tried to delay her. "If she goes back to the world of humans, she can tell of the moral choices of accepting virtuous actions and rejecting harmful ones. She can turn the minds of sentient beings."

The direct experience of other realms did indeed invest my mother with great spiritual authority when she taught of correct conduct and karmic cause and effect. No one doubted her words, not only because great lamas such as Tromge Trungpa had witnessed her corpse coming back to life, but also because she knew the whereabouts of buried coins and actions of the deceased before their deaths—things that she could not possibly have known without having been told directly by those she encountered as a delog. Later in her life one of the most generous contributors to her projects was a Tibetan businessman who had been an adamant non-practitioner of religion until my mother conveyed to him information about buried money from his deceased sister.

Delog Dawa Drolma's account here is as vivid as that of a tourist describing a country he or she has visited, yet hers is really a journey of consciousness through the pure and impure displays of mind. It begins when, as instructed by Tara, "I let my mind settle. In a spacious and extremely blissful frame of mind, I experienced a state of sheer lucidity. . . . I was fully aware of the fundamental condition of my mind in all its ordinariness. Because that awareness was unimpeded, it was as though I could hear all sounds and voices in all lands, not just those in my immediate environment."

When ordinary grasping and aversion and the ignorance of object–subject duality completely fall away, one experiences uncontrived, naked awareness—absolute, nondual, beyond concept, emptiness replete with all pure qualities and the potential to manifest as appearance inseparable from emptiness. This is buddha nature, obscured and unrecognized in sentient beings, but completely revealed in enlightened ones.

To provide benefit, enlightened beings spontaneously emanate realms of pure appearance such as Padmasambhava's Copper-Colored Mountain of Glory, Avalokiteshvara's Potala Mountain, and Tara's Yulokod. Practitioners who have purified their mindstreams and who have accumulated vast merit through their virtue can experience pure realms in visions, in dreams, or, as my mother did, as a delog. Her account is quite specific in its cosmological geography and detailed in its descriptions, yet it is clear that the realms she visited are the rich display of the nature of mind, experienced when meditation breaks through the limitations of ordinary perception.

The pure realms are the display of mind, but so also are the bardo state and the six destinations of rebirth. The difference is that the pure realms are the display of enlightened awareness, while the six realms and the bardo are the display of delusion and the projection of mind's poisons. The hell realm is a projection of hatred and anger and the nonvirtue of killing; the preta realm, a projection of avarice and craving; the animal realm, a projection of stupidity; that of the demigods, a projection of virtue tainted with jealousy; that of the gods, a projection of virtue tainted with pride; the human realm, a projection of a mixture of all five poisons combined with at least enough virtue to prevent rebirth in lower realms. Fortunate human rebirth is founded in a large measure of virtue and enables one to practice a spiritual path. My mother used to say, "No matter how difficult your life is as a human being, there is no comparison between the difficulties here and the miseries in lower existences."

Humans and animals share this world and with it a tendency to see things as very solid, substantial. When death separates the mind and body, and strips away the relative stability of form, the naked consciousness enters the after-death bardo state. If liberation is not attained early on during the pure display of what is known as the bardo of the true nature of reality, one's consciousness is propelled into the bardo of becoming, after which it will take rebirth in one of the six realms of experience according to one's karma.

꣓৹। As if in a dream or hallucination, beings float in and out of Dawa Drolma's perception like flakes of snow. In one instant she encounters an acquaintance enduring the most hideous torments of hell or a preta suffering the agonies of extreme deprivation; in the next she meets a virtuous person en route to a pure realm or a being in a god realm. Occasionally, she sees whole processions of hell or bardo beings leaving for the pure realms, shepherded by a great lama or practitioner who by the power of his or her altruistic aspirations has come to save beings. This is truly what is meant when we pray to "dredge the depths of cyclic existence and liberate beings."

Dawa Drolma is confronted by Yama Dharmaraja, lord of death, and along with Tara sings him a song of realization:

If there is recognition, there is just this—one's own mind;
if there is no recognition, there is the great wrathful lord of
  death.

In actuality this is the victorious one, the dharmakaya
   Samantabhadra:
We offer homage and praises at the feet of Dharmaraja.

Despite the fact that the realms of cyclic existence are in
the absolute sense empty in nature, mere projections of
mind's delusions, on a relative level the suffering of beings
trapped there is undeniable. As Dharmaraja and his minions
demonstrate again and again, no lies or pretenses mitigate
one's karma. One's life passes before one's eyes with every
good and bad deed clearly delineated; karmic results arise accordingly. Dawa Drolma's chilling descriptions of the horrible
consequences of killing and harming others clearly caution
one to avoid such actions. On the other hand, her captivat-
ing descriptions of the pure realms inspire one to practice
deity meditation and to realize the qualities of mind's pure
nature.

After death, even as karmic forces propel one's consciousness to rebirth in cyclic existence, if one has previously practiced well enough to have the presence of mind to invoke
one's meditational deity with faith, one is instantaneously
reborn in that deity's pure realm.

ॐ After her delog experience, Dawa Drolma made a
pilgrimage to Lhasa, where she conceived me with her consort, a high lama. She lived with her parents until I was
about four, then relocated to Tanp'hel Gonpa, a monastery
about a week away by horseback. A house with a beautiful
view was built high on a mountainside, and she lived there,
revered as a lama and a *dakini*, a female embodiment of wisdom and enlightened activity. She later gave birth to my sister, T'hrinlay Wangmo, an extraordinary child who was
eventually recognized as an incarnation of a wisdom yogini.
Both my sister and I were wild, willful children, and I still

sometimes feel overwhelming regret at the difficulties I caused my mother. She did not refrain from inflicting strict discipline, but she also affirmed that if I practiced dharma strongly and with pure motivation, I would be of benefit to beings. Her words deeply empowered my path.

In 1941 she died, shortly after giving birth to a baby boy, who himself died two years later. She was in her mid-thirties; I was eleven years old. Her body remained in meditation posture for some days, then collapsed, indicating that the consciousness had left. She was cremated on the roof of her house. Rainbows appeared, and five vultures, who in Vajrayana Buddhism symbolize the supreme perspective of the realized yogin, circled overhead. I am sure that she returned to the pure realms, but equally, I have no doubt that she also returned to the hell and preta realms to rescue whoever had a connection with her. She was absolutely fearless in her compassion.

I left Tibet in 1959, just ahead of the brutal Chinese consolidation of conquest. In 1982, after almost three decades without word from my family, I suddenly received a short letter from my sister in which she mentioned that she had the only copy of my mother's delog account. This was like a hook cast from Tibet to California, yet I could not seize it until five years later when China's political stance on Tibet had softened slightly. When I finally visited T'hrinlay Wangmo, she told me that the text had been confiscated but she had learned who had it. During the terrible years of the Cultural Revolution, when religious texts were used as toilet paper by the Chinese, she could do nothing, but as soon as she felt safe, she offered an exorbitant sum to obtain the account. Only a few pages were missing.

I did not want to take the original away from her, but the Chinese in the Szechuan capital of Chengdu would not allow me to photocopy it. Knowing I might have to smuggle it out, I had brought Tibetan books from the United States and listed them on my customs declaration. I added the delog account to my collection and had no trouble transiting the airport. A few years later, I returned to Tibet to give a copy to my sister. I still have the original, now more than sixty years old, taken down by a scribe in fine handwriting as Dawa Drolma told her story.

༄༅། There are other delog accounts—one by another female practitioner, Delog Ling Zha Chhödron, is quite well known. The Tibetan Library of Works and Archives in Dharamsala houses at least a dozen. Delogs were often women; some appeared to be ordinary laypeople, but the experience itself is a sign of great meditative realization, so they could not have been truly ordinary. Their narratives increased people's faith in the lamas' teachings about the unseen realms of existence.

I do not know if other accounts have been translated into Western languages. It is very fortunate that my connection with the excellent translator Richard Barron (Chökyi Nyima) and the very capable editor Mary Racine has brought forth the English translation of Dawa Drolma's account. Richard Barron is responsible for the lucid footnotes. Although the chapters were written with the three pure realms first and then the impure realms comprising a fourth chapter, the internal evidence of the text seems to indicate that the journey unfolded in the order published here: the Copper-Colored Mountain of Glory, the impure realms, Potala Mountain, and Yulokod. The final chapter, which was brought from eastern Tibet to the United States by my son, Jigme Tromge Rinpoche, in 1994, is a summary, primarily of Dawa Drolma's experiences in the impure realms. To render the English more readable, the text is a somewhat free prose translation of the original Tibetan verse, rather than a strict literal translation. The phoneticization of Tibetan forms is based on a system employed by Padma Publishing.

ༀ The delog experience is extraordinary, marvelous, even within the esoteric context of Tibetan schools of Vajra-yana Buddhism. Yet Delog Dawa Drolma's account has the power and immediacy of direct experience, and I trust that those who read it will find that the phenomena of the realms correspond to aspects of their own mind's experience. May her words inspire the highest spiritual attainment; may they guide whoever reads them to the dominions of the victorious ones.

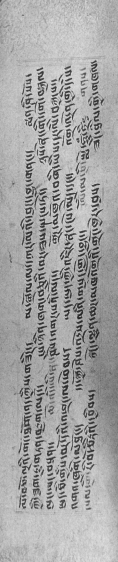

Folio 2 from the original handwritten manuscript of Chapter 5 recovered from eastern Tibet in 1994

COPPER-COLORED MOUNTAIN OF GLORY

THE PURE REALM OF PADMASAMBHAVA

1

The path of which I speak is a narrow passage, cramped
  and close.
So that those who desire liberation may enter the path to
  that liberation
I will expand a bit on this garland of healing advice
  concerning higher motivation.[1]

ॐ꣰ The accounts to be related here concern me, Dawa
Drolma, the daughter of Jigmed T'hrogyal of the Tromge
clan, a lama who lived in the region of Washul T'hrom. From
the time that I was a small child, I was endowed with a compassionate nature, unbiased faith, and pure vision. My love
was strong for all beggars and those less fortunate than I, and
I devoted myself to making offerings and giving charity.

I performed many intensive recitation retreats, completing, for example, hundreds of thousands of repetitions of the
Seven-Line Supplication.[2] Later on I was inspired by the dakini Dorje Yudron[3] and other deities of pristine awareness, as
well as by a bodhisattva dwelling on the eighth level of realization,[4] who took the form of a local god, the great divine
nyen of the north.[5] Although they did not fully relate the
past, present, and future to me, nonetheless I received an incredible number of prophecies that are relevant to our times.

೧೨೯| At one time the three *tulkus*,[6] as well as Jatrul[7] and others, traveled down into the valley to participate in an extensive ritual, an annual event held in a large felt tent. On the evening before they were to disperse, I had a vision that was partly a meditative experience, partly a dream. In this vision, three demons known as the "sisters of broken samaya"[8] came from the direction of Lashar Plateau, robbing the life force of beings on the three planes of conditioned existence.[9] The principal sister held a black silk banner and a noose; although she attempted again and again to loop them around my waist, my karmic deity, the venerable Tara, appeared in a youthful manifestation, her form brilliant white, and placed me within a protective fortified tent, so that the noose could not reach me.[10]

Later, I had a vision of someone approaching and striking me on the shoulder blades with a skein of colored wool the size of a small rock, then disappearing. This was a very negative experience, but again Tara intervened, saying, "Because of this, I must go to India to get some *kanadava* medicine from the secret treasury of the dakinis of Orgyan.[11] I will not return for four days. During that time, you should wear the clothing of someone such as your older brother Palchhen whose body is protected by guardian gods and keep your mind from wandering. On the evening of the fourth day, offer eighty *tormas* to dispel hindrances.[12] Then, as a sign that I have acquired the medicine, I will come as the sun blazing, unobscured by clouds, or surrounded by a violent wind."

During these four days I suffered intensely; the pain was so great that I could not tie my sash around my body. On the evening of the fourth day, the incarnate lama Tromge Trungpa performed a ritual of eighty torma offerings, and the three life-force-cutting sisters, delighted with the offerings, returned to their own abodes. A pleasant odor filled the felt tent from top to bottom, indicating that the medicine had arrived. I could taste an extraordinary substance with a very fine fragrance, and immediately my pains dissipated. I actually experienced this marvelous occurrence, which anyone could have witnessed for themselves.

At another time, I was suddenly struck down as though the hour of my death had certainly come. My precious root lama[13] and sole refuge, that gracious sovereign lord who is a treasure trove of compassion, vigorously performed a ceremony to recall my longevity force. As well, lamas of the illustrious Sakya lineage[14] performed supplication prayers, rituals to confer protection, the refuge ceremony of the glorious Hevajra,[15] and other ceremonies. At last the more overt pains were soothed, and the more subtle ones subsided into an experience of bliss and emptiness.

It was then that Khakyod Wangpo, the sovereign lord of a hundred buddha families, the incomparable and unique treasure trove of compassion, the flawless great Vajradhara[16] in actuality, guided me in a vision with his illusory form of pristine awareness. I conversed, as one person would speak to another, with dakinis of pristine awareness who had no physical bodies, and they gave clear answers to my questions, so that the obstacles to this girl's[17] life span were dispelled and I could benefit beings in accordance with my own capacities. It was prophesied to me that I would have to undertake recitation retreats on three deities—Amitayus, Samyak, and Vajrakilaya—in order to visit many nirmanakaya pure realms.[18]

The lord Tromge Kundun Rinpoche performed the empowerments for these three deities from the teachings of the great *terton* Laykyi Dorje.[19] My habitual ways of looking at things were simply swept away, and I was introduced directly to the unconditioned essential nature of intrinsic awareness, without confusion. I burst through to intrinsic awareness in all its nakedness, whereupon secret vajra words welled forth without interruption.[20] The venerable goddess, the exalted White Tara, graced me with a vision, and many meditative experiences of an unimaginable union of bliss and emptiness dawned in my mindstream.

꣠꣠꣠ It was the first year of the ancient sixty-year cycle, the wood male rat year.[21] During the waning phase of the moon in the eighth month, on the twenty-third day of the lunar calendar, there fell an important occasion commemorating the gathering of dakinis, an auspicious time for the renewed dissemination of the precious teachings of the secret mantra path.[22] On that day, we went to visit Chhogtrul Rinpoche. This girl persistently asked him about the dreams and meditative experiences of her early life, as well as later and more recent experiences. He seemed incredibly joyful and extremely pleased by these accounts.

I said to him, "According to a prophecy that White Tara made to this girl, I shall spend some six or seven days in a state of deep meditative stability, as though in a coma or in a state like death."

Chhogtrul Rinpoche and Tromge Trungpa both told me, in effect, "There is absolutely no need for this sort of talk. After spending no more than one day in a *nyungnay* fasting ritual, you feel hungry and thirsty.[23] Wouldn't it be better to remain in a naturally tranquil meditation hut, without many things to think of, relaxing easily in the key points of the stages of development and completion[24] and completing a few mantra repetitions?"

"But," I responded, "to remain for seven days in such a state would be of benefit and enormous importance for curing my illness." I pestered them again and again, asking, "Shouldn't I stay in my room with the door locked, taking no food or water at all?"

Tromge Kundun Rinpoche said, "Do nothing of the kind! If you want your illness to abate, you should perform extensive longevity rituals and ceremonies, and receive the empowerments for Vajrakilaya and the ablution ritual of the deity Bhurkakuta.[25] You should also ransom the lives of animals doomed to slaughter. If you wish to improve the welfare of beings, practice a ritual such as the one for leading beings from the six realms[26] found in the cycle of *The Natural Freedom of Enlightened Intent* of the peaceful and wrathful deities[27] and invoke the principle of supreme compassion by reciting the *mani* mantra[28] along with prayers of dedication and aspiration."

In this and many other ways he enjoined me, and although it would have been very good to follow his advice, I reiterated that in my opinion there was nothing to be done but what I had already described, and I made the decision to act accordingly, unable to procrastinate any longer.

On the twenty-fifth day of the lunar month I informed everyone around me of the situation. In the evening, the time of power,[29] when dakinis are gathered, seven quite special lamas and tulkus (the omniscient lama Tromge Kundun Rinpoche foremost among them) were joined by many of their students and attendants. This girl also joined the gathering. While I was there, my mind became much more lucid than ever before, and very special meditative experiences and states of realization arose in my mindstream. Within the hearing range of Tromge Kundun Rinpoche I recited in their proper order liturgical texts that I had never studied, the

Commands of the Mother Consort, as well as the feast offering and fulfillment ritual.[30] My mind was intensely joyful, and I felt I would never be happier than I was that night.

After the gathering broke up, I stayed for a short time in the presence of my precious lama. Using many ploys, both peaceful and wrathful, Rinpoche said over and over, "My girl, I urge you not to carry out this plan." However, it was of no use and so at last he said, "Since you are determined to do so, keep the following words in mind and never forget them. From now on, don't get caught up as you have in the past in the path of impure, rampant delusion. Settle without contrivance into the genuine nature of your mind, just as it falls in and of itself. As much as you can, generate faith in and pure view of your lamas and chosen deities, as well as love and compassion for all beings, who have been your fathers and mothers."[31]

With that, he honored me by personally giving me a full plate of the select portions of the feast offering. He intoned, "May you be placed under the protection of the lamas, the Three Jewels, and the great Orgyan.[32] Until you achieve enlightenment, may all obstructing and counterproductive conditions be pacified. May the uncontrived enlightened intent of the two aspects of *bodhicitta,*[33] the fundamental nature of reality, be born in your mindstream. May you be led on your path by the venerable goddess, the exalted Tara, and so accomplish inconceivable benefit for beings."

As he said these words, my faith grew so strong I felt as though I would burst into tears. I performed three prostrations and returned to my retreat house.

༄༅། Later I told Tulku Tromge Trungpa, "For a period of about five days, I will be as though actually dead. During that time none of the monks or students should go in or out of my room or walk back and forth much outside the door; they should not chatter or make other careless, disruptive noises. Remove all the foodstuffs that are in my presence, not leaving so much as seven grains of barley.[34] To purify the habitual tendencies, womb obscuration,[35] and stains of my body, wash me with saffron water that has been consecrated through the practice of Vijaya.[36] At that time, to provide a particularly auspicious condition, there should be a girl present named Drolma." (As it turned out, things took care of themselves, for a virtuous woman of pure samaya commitment named Tsult'hrim Drolma became my companion.)[37]

I continued, "To make it clear which buddha family is mine and to remove obstacles, wrap a blue cloth the color of the sky around my head.[38] Until I return to life, Kuzhab Rinpoche[39] will perform the offering of oblations to the five sisters of Lhaman Tsering.[40] Tromge Trungpa will perform one hundred feast offerings of the Queen of Supreme Bliss in the cycle of the *Commands of the Mother Consort*. In order to offset obstacles to my visions, the students and attendants should recite as much as possible the Seven-Line Supplication, the prayer Dispelling Obstacles on the Path, and the *vajra guru* and Tara mantras.[41] To protect me, bolt my door with a padlock and have someone wearing blue wrap the lock with a blue cloth. And to suppress and overwhelm the influence of bloodthirsty demons, seal the cloth with wax imprinted with the seal turned upside down.[42]

"Now have a change of clothing brought that is not made of animal skin or hide.[43] If I do not actually die but instead return to life, I shall want to rinse my mouth; for this, I shall need a vase full of clean rainwater collected during a shower of the medicinal rain of the seers, which comes about through the force of the blessings and aspirations of the Medicine Buddha Bhaishajyaguru.[44]

"If anyone asks what Dawa Drolma is doing acting like this, do not say anything specific, good or bad; merely acknowledge that I am neither decisively alive nor dead. Within five days summon my brother Palchhen, who lives with my family and kinspeople in the valley below, and tell him, 'Your sister is in such a state that she is neither alive nor dead. Come and see for yourself.' Everything that I have just specified, though it involves a little hardship, is very important, so please carry it out."

Tulku Tromge Trungpa and his attendants promised to observe to the letter the instructions I had given and to remain faithful to their commitment, and so I lay down on my bed to relax.

This girl had been told, "Let your mind settle in the natural state into which it inherently falls, without any discursive thought interrupting." Accordingly, I let my mind settle. In a spacious and extremely blissful frame of mind, I experienced a state of sheer lucidity. This was not the latent state of *kunzhi,* which is the mere absence of discursive thought.[45] Nor was I simply indulging in feelings of bliss, clarity, and nonconceptual awareness.[46] And I had not merely fallen into an endless playing out of my confusion. Rather, I was fully aware of the fundamental condition of my mind in all its ordinariness.[47] Because that awareness was unimpeded, it was as though I could hear all sounds and voices in all lands, not just those in my immediate environment.

On the morning of the twenty-sixth day of the lunar month, as the sun peeped over the horizon, I beheld the exalted and venerable Tara actually present before me within a mass of rainbow light, her form white like a vase of crystal. She held an arrow decorated with silk ribbons, with which she blessed me.[48]

From the direction of the Mountain of Glory on the subcontinent of Chamara, a rainbow of five parallel bands of colored light penetrated my meditation room.[49] Along this pathway came an escort of four young women dressed in silks and adorned with ornaments of bone. The dakini of the east, Goddess with Power over Longevity, was brilliant white and held a silk-beribboned arrow and a vase. The dakini of the south was Akyang Tara, the dakini of the west was Tara of the Turquoise Dragon, and the dakini of the north was Goddess of the North.

They placed me in a litter covered with variegated silk patterned in red and white. Immediately, the dakinis of the four classes and I joined together in chanting the Seven-Line Supplication and reciting aloud the vajra guru and mani mantras continuously. My mind expanded into a supremely blissful state, the essential nature of sheer lucidity in which I could not cling to anything as good or bad in the ordinary sense, like unborn space that is nothing at all in and of itself, yet with an absolutely unimpeded natural radiance. This harmonious and spontaneous meditative experience emerged as the inconceivable array of a cloud mandala, the entire vast range of pure experience.[50]

I then had the sensation of climbing higher and higher into vaguely defined space, more swiftly than a wild white-tailed vulture soaring into the heavens. As this dramatic experience unfolded like a shifting phantasmagoria, I suddenly found myself in a place that I did not recognize. In the center of a vast plain, so spacious and ethereal that it seemed the sky had fallen to the earth, stood a large rock face shaped like a heart. In every direction were mountains like weapons thrusting up into the sky, red as though sprinkled with blood. In the sky appeared a canopy of five-colored rainbow light. Peacocks, thrushes, and cuckoos soared and flitted about playfully. The air was filled with the sweet fragrance of an incense that had the power to transform one's perceptions. Covering the ground in all directions were flowers of five lovely hues—white, yellow, red, green, and blue. I experienced this realm as an actual place.

I also saw a very beautiful mountain, as blue as a sapphire. My mind was filled with unimaginable faith and pure view. I continuously repeated aloud prayers of guru yoga, the Seven-Line Supplication, and a supplication previously spoken to me by White Tara herself, and I made prostrations and mandala offerings.

This place was the Copper-Colored Mountain of Glory on the subcontinent of Chamara. About midway up the rock face, on a vast and spacious level area, stood the immeasurable mansion of Lotus Light.[51] The temple, an emanation of Padmasambhava's enlightened awareness, was fashioned of five kinds of precious jewels, a self-arising and spontaneously accomplished mandala. From without, the inside was brilliantly clear, and from within, one could clearly see out. Festooned with loops of rainbows, the hall had four sides and four gates and courtyards, within which were other temples, more than a thousand of them. Within these were hosts of *vidyadharas*[52] as well as dakas and dakinis.

This girl arrived at the eastern gate. There I met four women, who clothed me in a robe of variegated silk, shining like a rainbow. Then they left, although I had no clue as to where they went.

The woman who was the keeper of the eastern gate challenged me: "Who are you?"

I replied, "I am Dawa Drolma, a daughter of the Tromge clan in the human world."

"Why have you come to this realm?"

I humbly responded, "For the purpose of ensuring the

welfare of all beings, I seek an audience with Orgyan Tsokyey Dorje[53] and the hosts of vidyadharas, dakas, and dakinis on the Copper-Colored Mountain of Glory on the subcontinent of Chamara."

The dakini replied:

May you be blessed by Vajravarahi.[54]
May adverse circumstances and obstacles to your longevity
    be dispelled.
May you attain the empowerment of the deathless vajra.
And may you ensure the welfare of measureless numbers of
    living beings.

I then beheld the extraordinary spectacle of the marvelous eastern gate, a door made of crystal. Above it, in bas relief, were an image of a *tathagata*[55] and accompanying words that produced liberation upon sight. To the left and right of the door were blue turquoise dragons worked in jewels, twisting in clockwise spirals and holding various gems.

All of a sudden the dakini opened the door with a key made of white quartz crystal, about a hand's span in length and marked with self-formed symbolic letters, magical and mysterious. I walked inside and found a long flight of stairs formed of jewels. I ascended these and in an immeasurably large chamber found the regent Jampa Migyur on a small throne.[56] He wore a cloak of white silk and was adorned with many jeweled ornaments, his hair bound up in a topknot. In his left hand he was telling a *mala* of white crystal, each of the 108 beads being about the size of one's thumb.[57] Surrounding him was a retinue of many hundreds of dakinis dressed in robes of white silk, celebrating a feast of sensory pleasures. Vajra goddesses of activity dressed in blue robes offered the select portions of the feast in the four cardinal directions of the sky.

This girl performed three prostrations from the back row

of the assembly and prayed with such noble aspirations as came to mind. Approaching the lama, I offered my confession, purified myself by reciting the hundred-syllable mantra,[58] and performed the thirty-seven-point mandala of the universe.[59] To the right of the lama was a dakini, who inquired minutely into my past; I answered her, speaking directly but humbly. The lama seemed intensely delighted. I took part in the celebration of the feast.

༄༅། Then I was shown out and guided by a blue woman to another immeasurable mansion. Everyone present there was bathing a dakini of a family of the lower steppes of eastern Tibet.[60] I too received a ritual bath. On a lofty throne in the midst of us, on an especially high cushion of red silk, sat that lamp who illuminated the sutras and tantras,[61] that crown jewel of ten million vidyadharas, that peerless master, learned and accomplished, the omniscient Jamyang Khyentsei Wangpo.[62] His lustrous form was charismatic and youthful; he seemed about sixteen years of age. He wore the three formal monastic robes, and on his head was a hat symbolizing the three collections of scriptures.[63] In his hands he held a vajra and a bell.[64] He was surrounded by a retinue of more than a hundred dakas and yoginis.

As before, I prostrated, made offerings, and performed the mandala offering of the universe. I presented him a length of flawless white silk to request an audience[65] and made such prayers of aspiration as I was able. The lama seemed to have a very harsh and intractable character; he spoke not a single word and deliberately avoided looking at me.

༄༅། I left and went to another immeasurable mansion. The doorkeeper was a girl who could not have been more than fifteen years old. Although I did not recognize her, she showed as much joy and delight toward me as parents do upon meeting their child. Inside, on a low seat piled with bolsters of green silk, sat a woman named Yul-lha, a dakini from the region of Derge who was an emanation of the deity Vajravarahi.[66] Her hair was bound up with silk ribbons the color of the sky, and she held a small text of spiritual instructions. She was reciting the root verses of the *Intermediate State after Death*.[67] There were some sixteen dakinis in her retinue. I prostrated to her and offered incense compounded from white Indian sandalwood. I was given food seasoned with spices made from five nectars.

We spoke at length about events in the human realm. She continued, "You will find four staircases in a pavilion in the center of this region. Do not take the black staircase, for there lurks danger from vicious poisonous serpents and bloodthirsty demons. Instead, mount the green staircase."

᭓᭓᭟ With that I continued on my way. In another immeasurable mansion I came across a woman who seemed quite old, her hair faded to yellowish gray, surrounded by about two hundred dakinis. The dakinis were reciting texts from Karma Lingpa's cycle of teachings on the mandala of peaceful and wrathful deities and the *Stainless Confession Tantra*.[68] The principal woman held her breath in the vase-breath exercise.[69] When she exhaled her breath completely, she expelled many water-dwelling creatures such as water snakes, frogs, and fishes; from their corpses emerged white, yellow, red, and green rainbows, while their consciousnesses were drawn to pure realms.

This woman was in fact a dakini called Wangmo. After prostrating and making offerings, I approached her. She placed a mala of skullbone on my head and, laughing gently, questioned me for a short time as to who I was.

In yet another immeasurable mansion I came upon a white goddess, a dakini of peaceful energy, seated on a silk-covered cushion and dressed in robes of divine brocade, surrounded by a retinue of seven dakinis. I prostrated and made offerings to her. The dakinis were very sweetly singing a devotional prayer to invoke the energy of the exalted Avalokiteshvara and a prayer of aspiration that incorporated the six-syllable mani mantra. But here I fear becoming too wordy and will not write further of this.

In a very beautiful immeasurable mansion whose door faced the east appeared the dakini Yeshe Tsogyal. Her form was beautifully clad in robes of silk and adorned with various jeweled and bone ornaments, her wavy hair lustrously black. Her inexpressibly lovely form, a joy to behold, was surrounded by a retinue of a hundred thousand dakinis. They were celebrating the feast offerings of the guru principle, *The Gathering of Awareness-Holding Gurus*; the deity principle, *The Gathering of the Great and Glorious*; and the dakini principle, *The Queen of Supreme Bliss*.[70] I joined the participants in the feast offering, prostrating and making offerings to Yeshe Tsogyal, which delighted her. I humbly told her my personal history very clearly and in detail.

"Continue upward," she said, "and I will send someone to conduct you to an audience with your own uncle.[71] It will be difficult for you to pass, for you will find a very stern gatekeeper."

I came to a terrifying palace, the very sight of which sent a thrill of fear through me. Canopies of human skin were hung with ropes made of snakes. Dry skulls and fresh and desiccated human heads, the hair still attached, hung everywhere. The curtains and hangings were of black python skin.

In the center of all of this, on a throne the color of the blackest jet, sat a yogi named Pawo Namkha Odsal, his color a dark purplish black. His hair was bound up in a topknot around a vajra, on the tip of which was a small piece of inset turquoise. In his ears were hoops made of conch shell. He wore a white robe and held a large hand drum and trumpet made of a human femur. Very charismatic, irresistibly so in fact, he was surrounded by a retinue of six figures clad in long black cloaks. They were all extremely wrathful, with flowing black hair and dark, scowling expressions. I prostrated and made offerings to them, as well as prayers of aspiration.

ༀ Continuing on, I encountered a gatekeeper, a white-skinned woman clad in silks and ornaments of bone. Her name was Nordzin Dronma, and she had had a connection with me for many lifetimes.

ༀ In the center of an immeasurable orange mansion of the nature of light, seated on a very high throne of red crystal and cushions of varicolored silks, was the divine consort Mandarava,[72] her color dark red. She held an arrow tied with ribbons of silk in her right hand and a longevity vase in her left. She wore a short, pleated silk skirt and was adorned with jeweled ornaments. Surrounded by a retinue of one hundred dakinis of pristine awareness, she sang a melodious song of indestructible vajra music. I prostrated and made offerings as I had before and, prompted by Tara, recited a devotional prayer to her. An unimaginable sense of faith arose in me.

I stood up in the audience and approached her. The divine consort placed her right hand, holding the beribboned arrow, on my head and chanted:

> *Hung* On the northwest border of the country of Orgyan, . . .
> I supplicate you to approach in order to grant your blessings.
> Having sent your blessings to this excellent place,
> bestow the four empowerments on this excellent practitioner.
> Dispel obstacles of untimely death.
> Grant the accomplishment of immortality.[73]

ᢀᢀ| Further on I came upon a very fine, charming mansion. Twelve women acted as gatekeepers at the eastern door, twelve at the southern door, twelve at the western door, and twelve at the northern door. On the eastern side, the door and the doorkeepers were all made of crystal, on the southern side of gold, on the western side ruby, and on the northern side turquoise.

In the eastern direction were twelve goddesses whose purpose was to guide beings, in the southern direction twelve goddesses whose function was to demonstrate the path to liberation. In the western direction I saw twelve goddesses of the blazing fire element, and in the northern direction twelve goddesses who were victorious over the *maras*.[74] All of them wore robes of colors that corresponded to their respective directions.[75]

The lock on the outer gate, about the length of one's arm,[76] was made of gold. One of the dakinis opened the gate and sent me in. Then the northern door to the mansion was opened and I entered the building. The hall inside had 180 supporting columns, and 180 dakinis, dressed in silks and adorned with ornaments of bone, danced as they sang to musical accompaniment a song entitled "The Natural Freedom from Lower States of Existence":

Hri The uncontrived state free of conceptual elaboration is
the dharmakaya guru.ཿ

Supreme bliss is the sambhogakaya guru, lord of dharma.ཿ[77]

Born from a lotus is the nirmanakaya guru.ཿ

We prostrate to and praise the vajra holder of the three
kayas.ཿ

Your enlightened form is unchanging, the form of
Samantabhadra.ཿ[78]

Your enlightened speech is unimpeded and self-arising,
guiding living beings.ཿ

Your enlightened mind is unwavering and goes beyond
speech, imagination, and expression.ཿ

We praise you, O Lotus King endowed with enlightened
form, speech, and mind.ཿ

Great scholar of the exalted land of India, so compassionate
to Tibet,ཿ

Lake-Born Vajra free of birth, death, aging, and
decrepitude,ཿ

converting hordes of malicious bloodthirsty demons to the
dharma.ཿ

We praise you, O Venerable Padma T'hod T'hreng Tzal.ཿ[79]

Om ah hung vajra guru padma siddhi hung.ཿ

Maha guru padma t'hod t'hreng tzal la namo hung.ཿ

As they sang, I experienced immeasurable faith and joy.

༄༅། At another palace, I came upon a white-skinned
woman dressed in a shawl and skirt of white brocade and
holding a mala of red crystal. She was the nun Kunga
Monlam, otherwise known as the dakini Laykyi Wangmochhe.[80] She showed heartfelt joy toward me. Parting a hanging curtain with designs in silk appliqué, she led me to the
center of the palace. There we found her retinue of seven
dakinis, who placed a white cushion out for me to sit on.

Laykyi Wangmochhe herself placed a white longevity arrow
on top of my head, intoning:

> Om Pristine longevity without flaw,≋
> I summon this in the most sublime glory of the conjunction
>   of sun and moon.≋[81]
> Longevity of supreme bliss without transition,≋
> I summon this in the glory of the subtle essence of the body
>   of light.≋
> Continuous longevity without ordinary coming into or going
>   out of existence,≋
> I summon this within the indestructible vast expanse, eternal
>   and stable.≋
> Longevity that is stolen, robbed, broken, or impaired by
>   discursive thought,≋
> I summon this in the fundamentally unconditioned nature of
>   nonconceptual pristine awareness.≋
> Longevity based on confusion about the appearances of
>   samsara, nirvana, and the spiritual path,≋[82]
> I summon this within the natural condition of things as they
>   are atemporally and pristinely.≋
> If there is no cessation, there is nothing to grow older,≋
> and so I also summon longevity that is without cessation and
>   aging.≋
> If there is no birth, there is no one to die,≋
> and so I also summon longevity that is unborn and undying.≋
> Ah Ah Ah.≋

She continued, "How fortunate that you have come to
this pure realm from the ordinary world of humans. How
touching you are." And she wept. Then she called out to a
girl named Apal to accompany me, and I was led out.

༄༅། The venerable White Tara said to me, "Dawa Drolma, my girl, it was I who arranged for you to leave the ordinary world of human beings and who led you to this pure

realm. But now the time is not ripe for you and me to stay here on the Mountain of Glory.[83]

"There is a pure realm higher than this, endowed with the five kinds of certainty,[84] which is the sphere of experience of those dwelling on the tenth level of realization. There the sambhogakaya form of the Supremely Compassionate One,[85] surrounded by a retinue of innumerable masculine and feminine bodhisattvas, is teaching the tantra of *The Supremely Compassionate Lotus Lord of the Dance.*

"Above that is the pure realm of dharmakaya, free of conceptual elaboration. There dwells Guru Padma, none other than the natural self-manifesting appearance of the pristine lord protector,[86] giving spiritual teachings to a gathering in which the enlightened intent of the teacher and that of the retinue are indivisible, presenting direct transmission instructions that go beyond symbols and words and ordinary thought—the Great Perfection tantra of the supreme secret, entitled *Self-arising Intrinsic Awareness.*[87]

"Nowadays there is a dearth of the good fortune needed to contact these levels directly. So formulate the aspiration again and again to do so at some point. Do not speak of your having come to this realm."[88]

At this I felt such pain I thought my heart would break, such sorrow I thought I might lose my mind, such complete disorientation that I could not recall anything I might have been thinking at the time; my perceptions were confused and disoriented. Tears flowed as though my eyes would fall out. I thought to myself, "Even though I may now be able to gain an audience with Padmasambhava, I have no formal offering to present to him, no gold or silver, no mandala offering, not even a silk scarf."

Immediately Tara gave me a very long, spotless white silk

ribbon from her beribboned arrow. Because of my great doubt, I thought that the arrow would be diminished by this gesture, but Tara said, "It can never be diminished, so don't be so stingy." She added, "This is no place to start crying. Go to the Guru and ask him whatever you wish. Regardless of what he gives you, whether gold or silver or gems, do not take it away with you. Request that instead he bestow upon you a blue silk scarf marked with the images of the five nirmanakayas.[89] Also request that your karmic connections with him from previous lifetimes be awakened, that your actions to benefit beings be without bias or partiality, that you gain the ability to perceive beings directly in lower states of existence and to inspire them to virtue, and that whatever prayers of aspiration you make be accomplished."

ༀ྄| Then I saw yet another palace, made of red crystal with two adjoining wings, like coral-colored sleeves on a garment. No key was required to enter; instead, there was a red symbolic letter over the door. In the doorway stood a white-haired woman with a complexion as white as a conch shell. She had a full set of teeth and was called the Goddess with Power over Longevity. She conferred upon me a ritual for summoning longevity and gave me a cut crystal with six facets. I had the distinct impression, however, that I should not accept the crystal, and so I placed it on top of a mandala plate piled with rice arranged in patterns reminiscent of Indian motifs.

ༀ྄| Further along I came upon an immeasurable mansion so vast and lofty that its dimensions were beyond accurate measure. The roof peaks were adorned with gems. Inside I saw hundreds of umbrellas made of peacock feathers, silken victory banners, wall hangings of satin, canopies of brocade, loops and strings of pearls, unimaginable arrays of offerings, and the wealth of a great feast offering heaped like mountains, tumbling down like crumbling embankments, and swirling like an ocean of nectar.

In this mandala like the incomparable clouds of Samantabhadra's offerings[90] was a wealth of sacred samaya substances surpassing the wealth of the great gods of the Nirmanarati heaven.[91] Rays of light emanated in all directions without limit from an enormous throne of dimensions difficult to fathom, higher even than a three-story building. On the throne was a seat of three piled cushions covered in multicolored silk worked with designs of thousand-petaled lotuses.

Seated there was he who is the essence in whom all sources of refuge and all victorious ones unite, the powerful lord of the enlightened mind of all victorious ones, the union in a single form of the three qualities—wisdom, love, and energy—of all victorious ones of the ten directions, the sole chosen deity of the Land of Snows, the kingdom of Tibet: the Guru of Orgyan, Padma T'hod T'hreng Tzal, the deathless Lake-Born Vajra himself.

His form was white with a reddish tinge. In his right hand he bore a vajra, in his left a longevity vase within a skullcup filled with nectar. In the crook of his left elbow he held the trident of the vajra secret.[92] His two legs were loosely crossed in the posture of royal ease. He wore a cloak of satiny maroon silk, a skirt of red silk, a red formal monastic robe with designs in gold thread, and an undergarment of the white silk of the gods. On his head rested the lotus crown that brings liberation upon sight.

When this girl beheld the perfectly proportioned mandala of the great Orgyan's visage, I gazed on it insatiably. All of my usual vague perceptions spontaneously ceased, and I experienced an ineffable, inconceivable, and inexpressible state, like a mute person tasting cane sugar.[93] For a short while I rested in this state of mind, at once joyful and sad.

In the four cardinal directions around the great Orgyan were four bliss-granting dakinis of pristine awareness, wearing robes of varicolored silks, their illusory bodies like masses of light. They waved longevity arrows and longevity vases in the four directions while singing songs of praise.

To the right of the throne, on another high throne, sat the venerable master of compassion, the great threefold vajra holder,[94] the sublime guide Dechhen Dorje (also known as Drimed Khakyod Wangpo). He was the latest powerful manifestation of a series of holy incarnations over many lifetimes that included Srongtzan Gampo (the form in which the exalted Avalokiteshvara emanated as a spiritual king to protect the northern realm of Tibet, the Land of Snows), as well as Nub Namnying and Dagpo Daod.[95] Dechhen Dorje's physical appearance was even more impressive than before,[96] resplendent with the "victory banner" of the saffron monk's robes. He wore the cap of a scholar, pointed with long earflaps, and held a hand drum and a bell. In the four cardinal directions around him I beheld four white dakinis holding arrows with blue silk ribbons attached. In front of him was a dark blue dakini with a wrathful expression, wearing a sash of multicolored silk and holding an arrow with a blue silk ribbon.

On a throne to the left of the central one was someone who had transcended all activity, the realized master Jigmed Pawo (also known as Dza Konchhog), who was a rebirth of Lhatsun Namkha Jigmed[97] and who had been the heart son of Dzaga Chhogtrul Rinpoche.[98] He had a dark bluish complexion, was clad in flowing robes of silk, and wore a scholar's cap. In his hands he held a vase. He was a king among accomplished adepts who in his lifetime had come to the consummate realization of the four visions of the secret path uniting original purity and spontaneous presence[99] and whose mind was immersed in the state where ordinary phenomena fall away in the true nature of reality. In the four cardinal directions around him were four red dakinis wearing red silk robes, and in front of him was another dakini.

I also beheld a host of about ten thousand dakas, holders of intrinsic awareness, wearing hats of peacock feathers. The space surrounding them was filled with countless billions of goddesses making offerings, from drinking and bathing water to flowers and food. Some of them were holding vajras and bells, some small hand drums on sticks, some cymbals, some golden gongs, some conch shells, and some (in the four cardinal directions) trumpets of white, yellow, red, and green. The trumpets in the west were fashioned of coral and were blown by two dakinis wearing orange robes; I was told that they performed the special function of drawing beings to the secret vajrayana path. The thighbone trumpets were made entirely of human femurs, not of copper or brass.[100] About a hundred reed horns also resounded. There were some one hundred shrinekeepers in yellow robes, their left shoulders draped with the traditional piece of multicolored silk.

I asked one of the dakinis, "What is the group ritual being practiced here?"

She replied, "We are performing the ritual and offering ceremony of the *Eight Commands, the Gathering of Those Gone to Bliss,* which is the essence of the teachings of the early school of translation."[101]

At this, the many members of the assembly rose. I too, feeling embarrassed and afraid, rose and performed prostrations swiftly over and over. Moving closer, I placed the feet of the omniscient great Guru on the crown of my head. I offered him a mandala fashioned of precious metals and stones and a stainless length of white silk. The great Orgyan then placed his hand on my head, reciting the Seven-Line Supplication.

My paternal uncle, Khakyod Wangpo, began, "With power over longevity, your life shall be limitless . . ." and, while waving a longevity arrow, recited a liturgy for summoning the forces of longevity.

For his part, Dza Konchhog chanted:

The perception of pristine awareness is vividly clear.ঽ
The lamp for living beings is the torch of pristine
   awareness.ঽ
Supremely resplendent and majestic, radiantly luminousঽ
is the master who holds the mantra, the king of the mantras
   of awareness.ঽ
Aঽ P'hatঽ Aঽ P'hatঽ Aঽ P'hatঽ

I remained kneeling on a seat of white silk, crying and crying. The tears I shed collected like water on the crystal floor. At last, out of my overwhelming pain, I cried, "O precious uncle, you have forsaken sentient beings, particularly those of us who are your students and servants and who are the objects of your affection. While you, Uncle, have gone to a pure realm without leaving a trace, this girl feels greater pain than if her heart had been torn out. Your other students and servants feel this way too. Uncle, I pray to you from my heart. You simply must return to the human world for the benefit of beings. Until your enlightened embodiment reappears, this girl will not go anywhere. I have come here with deliberate intent. Having come, I have met with you; and having met with you, I have made my request. Let all that I ask of you have meaning, I beg you!" And I began to cry again, my eyes overflowing with tears.

Drimed Khakyod Wangpo showed his great affection by

replying, "What you, Dadrol, my niece, have said is certainly true, yet you should not be unhappy. Between me and the great Lama Orgyan there is not the slightest difference. Despite the conventional labels of 'birth' and 'death,' for me there is not, in the ultimate sense, the slightest erroneous notion of birth or death.

"All sentient beings who have had any connection—positive or negative—with me, this old man Dechhen Dorje, have been led to the Mountain of Glory on the subcontinent of Chamara, the pure realm of the victorious ones of the three kayas, like a flock of birds startled by a pebble thrown from a sling.[102] Even now, I give you my solemn word that those students and servants who are capable of supplicating me will become buddhas simultaneously.

"You who suffer on my account, be vigilant in your devotion, seeing the lama as the dharmakaya of buddhahood. Be vigilant in your compassion, understanding the six classes of beings to be your parents. Be vigilant in your practice of virtue, not tarnishing anything you undertake with selfish vested interests. Be vigilant in your mantra repetition and meditation practices, not falling under the eight worldly influences,[103] understanding the six-syllable mani mantra alone to be sufficient for your practice. Be vigilant in your formal practice, subsuming everything within your own true mind. Don't make mistakes! Don't make mistakes!

"As soon as you shed this human body, I will lead all of you to this pure realm like a goose leading her goslings. Just see if I don't, by the Three Jewels! When you return to the human realm, relate all of these messages to Tromge Kundun, to the households of the region, and to my dear students. Do as I say, for even if they were to meet with me directly I would have nothing further to tell them."

Saying this, he gave me a splendid portion of the food and drink of the feast offering. Performing three more prostrations, I left him.

༄༅། In a mansion of crystal with eight turquoise dragons holding gems in their claws and twining in the eight cardinal and intercardinal directions, I found a charming bed with pillows and bolsters, and there I lay down. A dakini served as my attendant. I had the impression that I slept for a short time, when I was awakened by the sound of a bluish green peacock calling, "A a u u e o am!"[104]

I immediately went back to the sacred Guru and had an audience as before. I made many prostrations and offerings. In my uncle's sacred presence, I again wept. "Uncle, not only have you left us, but now the sole lord of refuge for the hopeful ones you left behind is Tromge Chhogtrul Rinpoche. If the merit that allows us to rely on him runs out, our suffering will be greater than that of a blind person who lacks a guide and falls over a precipice. What can be done to ensure that there will be no obstacles to Rinpoche's life, so that he may fully carry out his mission to benefit beings and satisfy his retinue and students?"

Uncle Khakyod Wangpo looked concerned. "That is certainly a valid point," he said. "Tromge Chhogtrul will live for another eleven years. But since he may suffer from some slight illness before that time, it will help to perform a ritual for turning back the escort of the dakinis the same number of times as his age, offering an effigy of his body in the direction that the sun rises.[105] Then it is certain that he will live that long."

I asked, "When will you return?"[106]

He answered, "For the present I shall go to the pure realm

known as the Charnel Ground of Erupting Volcanoes to teach the *Heart Drop of Chetzun*[107] to those gathered there. Although much might be said of the manner in which my incarnation will be born after that, do not write these things down, for they require a seal of secrecy.

"Now then, my girl, it is dangerous for you to remain in this realm and you should not come here again.[108] Return to the human realm and be of benefit to living beings. Before three years are out I shall be reborn there once again."

Although my pain at being separated from my refuge was great, I made preparations to return. I chanted the Seven-Line Supplication aloud three times and made many specific prayers of aspiration to Padmasambhava, to my uncle, and to the Three Jewels. As a sign that I had visited the Mountain of Glory on the subcontinent of Chamara, I was given the name Khadro Sherab Chhödron (Dakini Who Is a Lamp of Spiritual Wisdom).

The many beings gathered there struck up music, and dakinis acted as my escorts. My body was staggering and my mind was filled with attachment, but there was nothing to be done. My tears fell uncontrollably as I made countless prayers of aspiration.

〰〰᠀ Then we headed back. The dakini Tsewang Barma met with me again. She bestowed on me seven nectar pills[109] and a dakini's jewel box fashioned of quartz crystal, one cubit square. Since I did not take this with me, she pronounced a fine prayer of aspiration over me:

> May the teachings of the buddhas spread.᠀
> May the lives of the lamas be stable.᠀
> May bliss and happiness come to living beings.᠀
> May all attain awakened buddhahood.᠀

I also met the dakini Laykyi Wangmochhe again. She gave me white silk, rice, bundles of incense, and other things, and I stayed with her a short time. She said:

> May bliss and happiness come to this girl.⊗
> May there be no obstacles for this girl.⊗
> May there be protection and refuge for this girl.⊗
> May this girl be capable of benefiting living beings.⊗

Then I met once more with the divine consort Mandarava. A woman with a wrathful countenance poured a nectar that looked like charcoal water from her alms bowl and offered it to me. Mandarava said:

> May sentient beings be endowed with happiness.⊗
> May they be free of all suffering.⊗
> May they never be separate from happiness.⊗
> May they realize the equality of all phenomena.⊗

Next I met with the *repa*[110] Namkha Odsal, who said:

> Precious bodhicitta:⊗
> Where it has not arisen, may it arise.⊗
> Where it has arisen, may it never diminish⊗
> but increase more and more!⊗
> *Om mani padme hung.*⊗[111]

Then I met with the dakini Yeshe Tsogyal. She gave me a whitish liquid that looked like sap. Although she sang a song connected with the mantra containing the name of Padmasambhava, I have not written it down. She offered the following prayer of aspiration:

> For this girl Dawa Drolma,⊗
> in the ordinary world of the human realm,⊗
> in the field of vision encompassed by her eyes,⊗
> while in her corporeal body:⊗
> In the east when she looks to the east,⊗

may she behold a crystal gatekeeper.॰
When she looks to the south, looks to the south,॰
may she behold a golden gatekeeper.॰
When she looks to the west, looks to the west,॰
may she behold a coral gatekeeper.॰
When she looks to the north, looks to the north,॰
may she behold a turquoise gatekeeper.॰
When she sings a song of the vajra guru mantra॰
may she behold Padma Jungnay.॰
When feast offerings are performed here॰
may the girl come to visit this realm.॰
May she guide those sentient beings connected to her,
     physically or verbally,॰[112]
to the subcontinent of Chamara.॰

She told me, "Come here on the days of the lunar month when the effects of one's actions are multiplied a hundred thousand times: the tenth, the twenty-fifth, and the fifteenth days and that of the new moon."

She added, "Depart today without crying," but as she accompanied me for 100 paces, she let her own tears fall. She remarked, "Other than the small distance that I have come today, I actually never go anywhere." After walking another 110 paces, I looked back at her. I was exceedingly attached to her, but she called out, "Don't be unhappy because of this."

Further on, I again arrived at the place where the dakini Wangmo dwelled. One of the gate guardians led me to her. Owing to our strong connection, I wept out of fear that we would be separated, and the dakini herself also shed a few tears. She gave me a handful of grain.

She said, "I am not free to escort you, but I do have a message for you to take back. There is no fault in your having decisively cut your ties with the human realm and come here. Should you find yourself unable to break free from the jaws of a cruel crocodile or a vicious poisonous snake,[113] cast this grain and say as you do so, 'This is from the hand of the dakini Wangmo.' "

Continuing down, I was met and escorted by eight daki- nis, including Yul-lha, the aforementioned dakini of the Derge region. As we discussed my account of the pure realm, we wept over and over. "For now, stay the night," she said. "If I can bestow on you an empowerment of three deities— Amitayus, Samyak, and Vajrakilaya—then you, O dakini, will become, for the special tulkus, lamas, spiritual friends, and holy incarnate tertons who are in the ordinary human realm, a noble dakini who will dispel obstacles to their long lives." But I did not have the time to receive this empower- ment.

As I continued, White Tara warned me against speaking any words of bad omen. I came again into the presence of Jamyang Khyentsei Wangpo. He deliberately appeared to be more cheerful than he had been before, and he gave a slight laugh. He folded his palms together toward me, and White Tara said things such as the following:

> Whether you fold your hands or not,
> whether you have faith or not,
> this rebirth of the venerable White Tara
> is going to the ordinary world of humans.

Further down, the regent Jampa Migyur sent an escort of five dakinis to meet me. In order to dispel my fear of the denizens of hell, he gave me a blessing cord with a vajra carved from a sheet of slate and a scorpion-shaped knot carved in stone. He recited prayers of aspiration such as the one beginning "Precious bodhicitta . . ."[114]

As I continued on, White Tara said, "Well now! You haven't brought with you the dakini's jewel box made of crystal that we two were meant to carry back with us, so what is the point of bringing this stone knot, which is not necessary?" And so I let it fall to the ground.

꩜ Then in the lee of a rock face I saw a pure realm born of great aspiration, a vast palace of crystal. On the eastern gate was a lock of crystal about the size of my sleeve. To the right and left above the gate were two images of Amitayus. In between these I saw the six-syllable mani mantra written in three scripts one above the other: Tibetan, Lantza, and Wardhu.[115] There the dakini Yul-lha (whom I had met previously) and I encountered a girl of the Gya Chhagla family named Adam. She and Yul-lha were very joyful, kissing and embracing one another around the neck just like people in the ordinary world.

On a high throne inside the palace sat a lama of advanced age with a white beard. On a throne off to one side in front of him sat the sister of my father, Tromge Jigmed T'hrogyal; her name was Ashey Drolma. A woman with her hair bound up in a turban was asking many questions of both of them concerning the Buddhist teachings. There were about twenty thousand other women there, both laywomen and ordained nuns; all of them held metal butter lamps and chanted prayers of aspiration.

As I moved closer, Ashey Drolma said, "Take the following message to Jigmed T'hrogyal: 'I have been reborn in this realm of great aspiration. Both our parents have taken rebirth in Zangri Kharmar,[116] where they are benefiting beings as powerful tantric practitioners. Your name when you were little was Yudra Nyingpo; what you are called now is not clear to me, but you have committed both virtuous and harmful actions in this lifetime. While it is difficult not to perform such a mixture of actions as an ordinary mortal in cyclic existence, the important thing is that you have for once attained a human birth. The time is ripe to realize the potential of this, so recite the six-syllable mantra and do not fail to go into retreat occasionally. Then without doubt you will be reborn on the Mountain of Glory on Chamara immediately upon passing from this life.' "

I too made fervent prayers of aspiration.

ॐ। This, then, was my brief vision of the Mountain of Glory. I, a humble daughter of the clan of Lama Tromge, Dawa Drolma by name, died for a period of five days and experienced visions of the Mountain of Glory, Potala Mountain, and other realms. These accounts are not embellished with the words of the learned, nor adorned with the stylistic devices of classical poetry, nor fitted to the rhythms of proper meter. But neither have I made the mysterious words of the dakinis unintelligible.

These are the rambling, mad ravings of this girl herself, put down in writing by the incarnate Nyag Trulpa[117] just as I spoke them on top of Mani Tashi Pass in the region of T'hrom. I confess whatever faults they contain to the hosts of dakinis and dharma guardians, and may the virtue be cause for all those who hear even my name and who are devotedly interested in these pure visionary experiences to be reborn on the Mountain of Glory on the subcontinent of Chamara.

Good fortune, good fortune, good fortune!
Sarva mangalam—may everything be auspicious.

REFLECTIONS IN THE CRYSTAL MIRROR

THE SIX IMPURE REALMS OF BEING

2

Homage to Avalokiteshvara, exalted lord of the universe.

Your thousand arms are the thousand universal monarchs;
your thousand eyes, the thousand buddhas of this fortunate
    aeon.
You appear in whatever way is necessary to tame beings.
I prostrate to the exalted and sublime Avalokiteshvara.

I prostrate to her who protects us from the eight fears;[1]
I prostrate to her who guides us on the path to higher
    realms;
I prostrate to her who leads us to liberation.
I prostrate to Tara, with whom all connection is meaningful.

Their glorious forms unite all buddhas;
they are the very essence of the vajra holder;
they are the root of the Three Jewels.
I prostrate to the lord gurus.

By paying homage, making offerings, confessing,
rejoicing in others' merit, exhorting teachers to teach, and
    beseeching buddhas to manifest in the world,
whatever small virtue I may have accrued
I dedicate to unsurpassable supreme enlightenment.

Now Kundun Rinpoche, who has the vision of the
    Buddhadharma,
the two extremely gracious tulkus,[2]
the kind parents who gave me birth, and others
have urged me over and over, until I cannot ignore them,
and so I have written what is merely a drop in the ocean.

I, this humble girl named Dawa Drolma,
have given rise to pure motivation and entered the door of
    the dharma.
I have abandoned bad behavior and harmful, nonvirtuous
    acts.
I have made as many offerings to the Three Jewels as possible
and given in charity to beggars in whatever way I could.
I have made every effort to practice virtue.
Having cast off bad attitudes, I exert myself only in
    compassionate ways.

Some say, "Hers is a fortunate rebirth,"
and place themselves in the ranks of my faithful and devoted
    students.
Others say, "She's neither a god nor a demon."
However they explain me, it is difficult to take what they say
    as the truth.

In any case, I am a girl with few wants and needs.
I have no hopes of gaining renown.
I do not have the strength to carry the burden of a heroine
    seeking a lofty station.
I do not yearn for wealth or seek to gain even a thread.
I have no wish to preach, and lack a clever mouth and witty
    tongue.

Even so, with perfectly pure and altruistic mind
I feel I might influence the minds of a few beings,
and so I'll tell of a noble path, infallible and straight.
If you take this as true, it will be the greatest kindness you
    can do yourself,
for by making moral choices, you ensure your own welfare.
Therefore, listen well to these words of mine!

This is my story of dying and journeying to hell.
Revered lamas of high station,
rulers with great power and influence, seated on their
    thrones,
and wealthy guardians of fortunes, who manipulate happiness
    and hoard material wealth—
when they die and go to the realms of hell,
there are no multitudes of monks gathered in pomp and
    splendor,
no parades of soldiers with swords and weapons,
no great stores of food or wealth for making secret bribes.
Lofty status, ruthless might and power,
the wealth of the rich, the lovely bodies of the beautiful,
artful wit, and clever explanations
cannot beguile or fool the lord of death.
Has anyone in this human realm not died but stayed on?
Has anyone not been separated from family and friends?
Have anyone's acquisitions not been left behind?
Has anyone not fallen from a lofty height?
Better for you all if there were such people!

Though we speak of hell as somewhere far away, it is not.
Though we speak of the *bardo*[3] as somewhere else to go, it is
    not.
Death haunts us like our shadow follows our body.
If you are mindful of your inevitable death, you're the
    cleverest of all.
When the time comes to die, do parents and children,
spouse, relatives and friends, wealth and possessions alike
offer the slightest benefit or refuge? Look and see!
They do the greatest harm in sending you to lower realms.[4]
What, then, is of benefit? The infallible Three Jewels.
If you maintain a noble, virtuous mind and recite the six-
    syllable mani mantra,
you will not enter the path to lower rebirths in cyclic
    existence,
but gain the state of unsurpassable, complete enlightenment.
Om mani padme hung hri.

Do not fail to grant us refuge, O gurus and Three Jewels.[5]
Do not withhold your compassion, exalted Avalokiteshvara.
Be our refuge protectors, exalted goddesses white and green.[6]
Show us the path to liberation, O victorious ones and your
    heirs.
Om mani padme hung hri.

In the empty sky and empty earth of the bardo state between
    death and rebirth,
one has neither father nor mother to turn to for refuge.
In this dreary, strange place,
ordinary worldly beings wander, broken in spirit.
Om mani padme hung hri.

〰️⟩ Now I will tell of my visionary experiences. I, the girl
Dawa Drolma, was moving upward through an unfamiliar
and terrifying defile, when I met one Sherab Dronma, a
daughter of the family of Raga Shag, one of the ministers of
the Lhasa government. Because she was an incarnation of
the deity Vajravarahi, all those connected to her by having
shared with her or having received possessions or food from
her would be led to the pure realm of Chamara. Therefore,
she had appeared in lower realms of rebirth and had led
about one hundred million beings away with her. When I
encountered her, she was singing the mani mantra to an
extremely lovely melody, arousing such faith as brought tears
to the eyes of all present.

Both the exalted goddess White Tara (the deity with
whom I have a personal karmic connection and who has
guided me for many lifetimes) and Sherab Dronma manifested in seemingly ordinary forms. They behaved lovingly
toward one another, like a mother and child meeting. Toward me, moreover, Sherab Dronma acted in what seemed a
devoted and respectful manner. Then she sang the following
song:

Om mani padme hung hri.
There are five paths: white, red, blue, green, and yellow.
You, girl, know which path to take.
White Tara, lead her on that path!
The white path leads westward to the Realm of Bliss,
the pure realm of the buddha Amitabha.
The red path leads to Chamara,
the pure realm of Padmasambhava.
The blue path leads to Potala Mountain,
the pure realm of the exalted Avalokiteshvara.
The green path leads to Yulokod,
the pure realm of the exalted, venerable Tara.
The yellow path leads to the upper Realm of Flowers,
the pure realm of the regent Jampa Gonpo.
If you cannot decide which to follow,
there is little point in wandering in the bardo after death.
You, Dawa Drolma, know where to go.
May you reach the realm you seek.

I am an incarnation of Vajravarahi.
There are no lower states of rebirth for those connected to
    me by speech or touch.
From the Mountain of Glory in Chamara,
go to the world of the human realm.
May you be granted the blessings to undertake the path to
    liberation.

She continued, "It may be necessary for you, my girl, to
return to the human realm. But being only sixteen years of
age, your mental capacity has not developed fully, and having taken rebirth as a woman, you will have little authority.
Since sentient beings in these degenerate times will be hard
put to believe that your accounts are true, the benefit you
can bring them will be diminished." Tears fell profusely from
her eyes out of pity for me.

White Tara, who was guiding me on my path, seemed
slightly displeased by these words. She responded:

Ordinary worldly girls and this one are not the same,
for she is an emanation of White Tara.
She is a girl with a virtuous mind.
She is a girl with compassion.
She is a heroine with a courageous mind.
She is a dakini attested to in prophecy.
She is the niece of four lamas.

The stainless Khakyod Wangpo has departed to Chamara
   for a time;
this girl went to that realm hoping to meet with him.
She came to this place without attachment to her kind
   father;
she came to this place without attachment to her mother;
she came to this place without attachment to possessions,
   food, or wealth;
she came to this place without attachment to friends or
   servants.

Inseparable from lord Manjughosha,[7]
the lord protector, the activity emanation of a thousand
   buddhas,
is the refuge lord, great Sakya Sodnam Tzemo.[8]
His emanation in the form of a spiritual friend,
the excellent incarnation Lama Tromge Chhogtrul,
tried to delay her over and over, saying, "Don't go!"
but she would not listen and came to this realm.
She also encountered unfathomable realms of pure vision.
If she goes back to the world of humans,
she can tell of the moral choices of accepting virtuous
   actions and rejecting harmful ones.
She can turn the minds of sentient beings.
She can accomplish immeasurable benefit for them.
She can tell of her visions in these realms.
She can visit this realm again.
So there is no need to treat her with pity,
and you needn't feel unhappiness in your heart.

Then we moved on.

འཇའ། In the entrance to the long and fearful passage of the bardo was a personal student of Tromge Kundun Rinpoche, one Lama Gyajam. His hair was bound up in a topknot, and he wore a shawl and skirt of white cloth. Though I had strong hopes of meeting with him, we did not make contact, and soon I went on. I asked the compassionate mother of the victorious ones: "That lama of ours, the realized Gyajam—from what place, what direction, did he come? And for what purpose?"

The goddesses White Tara and Green Tara replied:

> That realized and especially exalted one named after
>   Manjughosha[9]
> has relied upon a gracious and extremely compassionate
>   lama.
> Because his karmic connection was great, he developed
>   perfect realization;
> because his exertion was great, he practiced the dharma
>   courageously;
> because his compassion was great, he came to teach the
>   dharma in the bardo.
>
> *Om mani padme hung hri.*

འཇའ། There is something more to relate: Hundreds of beings swirled upward like a blizzard; thousands more descended like a heavy snowfall. They cried out, their voices like the sound of a thousand dragons. A year's rainfall of tears fell from their eyes. From the summit of the sandy pass between life and death down to the great plains of burning iron in the hells, their numbers were immeasurable, like the grains of sand of the oceans. They were without rest or leisure, like ewes mixed with lambs.[10] Their suffering was unfathomable, like that of a fish on dry land. Like someone trying to climb a hill of sand, they had no chance of escape.

Like someone thrown into a fiery oven, they had no means to
withstand this pain. Like someone hallucinating water in a
mirage, they experienced the confused appearances of their
karma. Compassionate and exalted goddess, guide these beings who are experiencing such chaotic effects of karma!

   Om tare tuttare ture soha.

絪| On a vast, empty plain in the bardo, the daughter of
Tromge Kunga Dargyay, Lozang Drolma by name, was wan-
dering. Her suffering was neither very great nor very slight.
She gave me the following message to relate:

> Tell this to the members of my family:
> If you really feel that your daughter is suffering,
> a single recitation of a mani mantra would be of great
>   benefit.
> If you can manage to recite the *Sutra of Liberation,*
> as many mani mantras as possible,
> and the *Stainless Confession Tantra,*
> I can abandon this bardo body
> and attain rebirth as a human with pure samaya.[11]

With a compassionate mind, I called out the six-syllable
mantra to her from afar, and she was gone, carried away like
a feather on the wind.

   Om mani padme hung hri.

絪| On the very high, sandy pass between life and death,
there was an extremely bleak plain, the vast gray steppe of
death. The river of the dead was a turbid brown, with no
ford, only wildly tossing waves. The fearsome six-arched
bridge of the dead chilled my blood. The terrifying messen-
gers of Yama, lord of death, were extremely fierce and raven-
ous. Without a protector in the land of death, sentient beings are so helpless!

   Om mani padme hung hri.

꧁ Aga, the daughter-in-law of the Gyaten family of T'hromt'hog, was in that fordless brown river of the dead, suffering unimaginable pain. This was the end result of her having offered unclean tea to gatherings of many monks. I sang the mani mantra, and Tara saved her, pulling her out of the turbulent brown flood with a beribboned arrow.

꧁ I continued downward to a terrifying place. There was no illumination, but such a gloomy darkness that I could see only an arm's length in front of me. A rain of fire fell from above. Such ground as there was consisted of burning iron. Molten metal flowed in all directions, and various weapons were strewn everywhere. The bodies of the beings there were about one hundred fathoms in height, their skin an inky black. They cried out with a constant din, like a hundred ewes meeting their hundred lambs, "Alas! Alack! O woe! Ah! O Father! O Mother! Help me! Oh, how it burns!"

This chaotic and terrifying apparition seemed to disperse at a certain point.

꧁ In the middle of another vast plain stood a black iron throne about the size of a three-story house. On it was seated Dharmaraja,[12] lord of death. His form a dark purplish brown, he was terrifying, wrathful, and fierce. His eyes, shining like the sun and moon, were bloodshot and flashing like lightning. There were warts on his cheeks and other parts of his face. On his upper body he wore the fresh hide of an elephant, around his middle the flayed skin of a human being, around his lower body a skirt of tigerskin. He was adorned with silk garments and many ornaments of bones and jewels. On his head was a crown made of five dry human skulls. In his right hand he bore a crosshatched board of fate, in his left the mirror of karma.[13] He was seated in a cross-legged posture. The brilliance radiating from his body was unbearable to look at.

In front of Yama stood Malevolence, a minion with a serpent's head, holding a mirror. To Yama's right was Pride, with a lion's head, holding a tribunal drum. Behind Yama was Destiny, with a monkey's head, holding a balance. To Yama's left was Awa the Ox-Headed, holding scrolls. Surrounding them were countless millions of minions of the lord of death emanating in forms with the heads of numerous animals.

Both White Tara and I, the girl, performed three prostrations and offered the following hymn of praise:

> If there is recognition, there is just this—one's own mind;
> if there is no recognition, there is the great wrathful lord
>   of death.
> In actuality this is the victorious one, the dharmakaya
>   Samantabhadra.
> We offer homage and praises at the feet of Dharmaraja.
>
> If there is recognition, there is buddha Vajrasattva;
> if not, there is Malevolence with a serpent's head.
> In actuality this is enlightened mind, with anger totally
>   purified.
> We offer homage and praises to the great minion holding
>   a mirror.
>
> If there is recognition, there is buddha Ratnasambhava;
> if not, there is Pride with a lion's head.
> In actuality this is enlightened mind, with pride totally
>   purified.
> We offer homage and praises to the great minion holding
>   a tribunal drum.
>
> If there is recognition, there is buddha Amitabha;
> if not, there is Destiny with a monkey's head.
> In actuality this is enlightened mind, with desire and
>   attachment totally purified.

We offer homage and praises to the great minion holding
a balance.

If there is recognition, there is buddha Amoghasiddhi;
if not, there is Awa the Ox-Headed.
In actuality this is enlightened mind, with envy totally
purified.
We offer homage and praises to the great minion holding
scrolls.

They know no virtue or evil, these wrathful minions of
death.
May those sentient beings who have done nothing,
accumulated no evil karma,
without being led into paths impossible to escape from and
impossible to bear,
be reborn in a pure realm without error and without fear.

Dharmaraja smiled slightly and replied, "Well now, well-
spoken daughter from the human realm, what sort of positive, virtuous karma have you accumulated? What sort of
negative, evil karma have you accumulated? Speak honestly,
for it will not help to tell a lie!"

White Tara stood up, offered three prostrations to Dharmaraja, and said, "I have something to say on her behalf."

"Very well," he replied.

"This girl is a daughter of the family of Lama Tromge,"
she said. "As for her virtues, she makes whatever offerings
she can to the Three Jewels, regarding them as superior to
her. She has great compassion and does not disparage bad
people, mendicants, or beggars as her inferiors. She is very
generous, sir. Although she has not practiced the Buddhadharma a great deal herself, she has caused others to practice
and encouraged them in virtue. She always has great faith,
devotion, and bodhicitta. She has never committed a single
harmful or nonvirtuous act, my lord."

When she had submitted this, Yama said, "Well, now! The serpent-headed one will look into his mirror to see whether this is true."

The serpent-headed minion gazed into the mirror and said, "The image is like the sun coming out from behind the clouds." The lion-headed one beat the tribunal drum and pronounced, "The sound is sweet." The monkey-headed one weighed matters on the balance and declared, "Her virtue is overwhelmingly predominant; there are scarcely more than one or two harmful acts." Finally, the ox-headed guard glanced at the scrolls and said, "Just a minute! Haven't you committed some harmful actions, like smashing birds' eggs on the ground or showing too much willful temper?"

At that, Dharmaraja chuckled and said, "Ho, ho! Well, my girl, even though you're a compassionate one, heavy are the faults of evil people. If I were to punish some and not others, as I am king over evil deeds I would certainly be forced to experience the consequences of my own dereliction of duty. So for now I will send you back to your own realm once more, but you should confess your harmful acts and take care to be as virtuous as you can. Hold in your mind the scenes of hell, the messages from those who have passed away, and these words of advice from Dharmaraja. Recount them to others as well, encouraging all to practice virtue."

ॐ৷ Looking around, I beheld a daughter named Bilima from the region of Zurpa. A black snake as thick as the trunk of a pine tree was coiled around her body from head to foot, as though she were wrapped in a blanket. Minions of Yama shouted and bellowed, "Ha, ha! Ho, ho!" making an ear-shattering din. Her copious tears swirled like an ocean, and I heard her cry, "O Father, Mother, help me!"

The minions cried:

O wicked girl who kills snakes,
there is no point in crying to your father and mother.
This is the result of actions you yourself committed.
There will be no escape for a thousand aeons!

This was the end result of her having killed a snake while reaping barley in the fields. Her old mother had been afraid of the consequences of this act and had said to her, "You demoness, don't cry—confess this act!" The daughter had burst into laugher, and this rebirth was the result.

There was also a girl named Palkyid from the district of Nyagrong. Yama's minions had placed an iron sieve above her, through which they poured red-hot, boiling molten metal from one end of her body to the other. With the sounds of sizzling, her flesh and bones were seared and burned. She whimpered, unable to cry aloud. The minions shouted, "O wicked girl, in the ordinary human world you dawdled on the periphery of a gathering of ordained monks, and began smiling and flirting with them. Your hem, the edge of your garment, stirred up dust. One monk said, 'Don't behave like that—don't accumulate bad karma!' But you didn't listen to him, and what is happening to you now is the end result of your having upset these members of the sangha. There will be no chance of being freed for a thousand aeons."

The compassionate mother of the victorious ones waved a silk-beribboned arrow; I, the girl, recited the mani mantra to a melody. Freed from that low state, Palkyid took rebirth in the realm of her prayers, but it seems she still had to experience some of the results of her actions.

Om mani padme hung hri.

༄༅། Then I saw an old woman from the region of Tro, Anag by name. As boiling molten metal was poured into her mouth, her body burst asunder from head to foot. I saw her undergo this kind of suffering over and over. This, I was told, was due to her having poisoned a lama.[14]

Dingla of the region of Aso, and Khargya and others—most of the people of that region, in fact—were wandering in the bardo. Rinchhen Dargyay was also wandering there. One Nyima Holeb had been reborn in the Reviving Hell.[15] There were also about ten people from Aji. Some had been reborn in hell realms, some in *preta* realms.[16]

Among them, one named Abo had a head as large as a large clay pot and a horribly deformed body. His mouth was as small as the eye of a needle and his esophagus the width of a horsehair, while his stomach was as large as a whole city. His fingernails pierced through his clenched fists three times. He found nothing to eat; tongues of flame poured out of his mouth. He was experiencing unimaginable suffering.

I asked, "What action led to this man's suffering?" I was told that he had never made offerings to the Three Jewels as his superiors and had given little charity to beings in lower states of existence as his inferiors. He had never offered more than a small amount and then only with avarice for fear of running out of food.

An acquaintance of mine, one Atar of the Tanpa family of T'hromt'hog, was there. His message to his mother and close relations was, "Do not give up on your practice of virtue, of reciting mani mantras and the ritual of Akshobhya,[17] and of making donations to large assemblies of monks."

Tashi Dondrub of the Nag family had also taken rebirth there and was suffering unimaginably. I asked my companion Tara, "What acts did this man commit that led to this result?"

She replied, "Not guarding his samaya commitments and acting with arrogant selfishness, thinking, 'Will I get this?' and 'Will I get that?' "

He gave me the following message for his household: "Please, for my sake recite seventy million mani mantras and the *Sutra of Liberation,* confess your harmful actions, and offer prayers of dedication in large gatherings."

Gyashod Atsang had been reborn in a preta realm. An inconceivable number of others, both known to me and unknown, had also been reborn there. This realm was horrifying. The beings were extremely demoralized, because they could never find anything to eat or drink. Their hair bristled upward, their bodies were emaciated, their mouths were like the eyes of needles, their throats like horsehairs, their bellies like whole countries, and their limbs like stalks of grass. Their nails were very long, piercing through their hands nine times.

The majority of pretas had in their hands some spittle dedicated to them by Jamyang Khyentsei Wangpo,[18] but they would have to suffer for hundreds or thousands of years before they could open their mouths and lick a bit of it up. They would not find any comfort beyond this brief respite. In their suffering, they all cried, "What shall I eat? What shall I drink? I'm hungry! I'm thirsty! Alas, alas! Alack!"

The guardians of the preta realms set out various articles of food and wealth, then took sharp swords in hand and glared balefully. Driven by hunger, the pretas came to steal this food and drink, only to have their bodies hacked with these swords as they cried out in shock.

ༀ། Demigods were experiencing the intense suffering of strife with the gods dwelling on the slopes of Mount Sumeru.[19] They were unbearably envious of the splendor and

wealth in the god realms and of the flirtatious play of goddesses singing and dancing, but they only suffered the unimaginable pain of defeat at the hands of the gods. The gods
threw discuses with sharp spikes, as well as arrows and tri-
dents, and employed drunk elephants with wheel-shaped
weapons mounted on the ends of their trunks. The demigods
experienced the inconceivable suffering of being killed and
maimed. They also battled among themselves, with the ear-
splitting sounds of "Kill, kill!" and "Strike, strike!" resounding like the roar of a thousand dragons.

Even I myself was terrified by what I witnessed in that
realm. For having dashed a bird's egg on the ground, it was
necessary for me to pass under all the weapons; but I supplicated the bodhisattva of supreme compassion and the venerable goddess one-pointedly, and sang the six-syllable mantra
three times, whereupon it seemed to me that the sounds
gradually became softer.

About five thousand people of the region of Chamtring
and an indeterminate number of Chinese people had taken
rebirth in this same realm. There also seemed to be many
aristocrats, foremost among them Lozang Tendzin, a general
of Chamtring. An inconceivable number of people had been
reborn there, among them the Wanggyal family and the
Dugtza clan, the majority of whom who had died by the
knife.

ༀ༈ Further on, in a park full of flowers, I found an extremely old god, suffering nothing but pain. Some companions approached and cast flower garlands at him, saying, "As
soon as you discard your physical body, may you be reborn in
the human realm, practice the ten kinds of virtuous actions,[20]
and be born once again in this god realm." With this, they

scattered blossoms. He experienced unimaginable suffering, as though his heart had burst and his body had melted into the sand.

The length of a god's life can be calculated from the fact that about seven thousand of our human years is a single week for the gods. In the week before their death, they suffer agonies far worse than those of the worst hell of ceaseless torment. As their karma is exhausted, due to thoughts tainted by emotions such as pride, they actually see the place of their future rebirth in a lower state of existence. That causes them more severe suffering than committing suicide by hurling oneself into an open pit of fire.

Om mani padme hung hri.

ༀༀ| I continued on and met Kardo of the Getsay clan in a hell realm. There, inside a huge iron house of enormous dimensions, he was gathering earth, rock, grass, and wood (though I questioned the necessity of his actions), and especially turquoise, coral, crystal, lapis, gold, and silver. Then the hordes of minions of Yama piled all the wealth and the earth and rocks on top of his body. He cried out in pain. Whenever he tried to escape, he was stopped. Afterward, he had to watch the precious stones and metals being scattered like feathers in the wind, and once more his mental suffering intensified. Then, as before, he amassed wealth and food, and again was crushed by them, and so he spent every moment experiencing these alternating forms of pain.

I asked, "What action is this the result of?"

Tara told me, "This is the result of his having coveted everything he laid his eyes on, of having had ill-will for everyone he heard, of having had nothing but wrong views about everything he thought of. This is the result of not practicing virtue, but of engaging in nonvirtuous and harmful actions, including carrying an ornamented mala while being distracted by gossipmongering and idle talk."

Kardo gave me this message to bring back: "To Tsagdi, the daughter-in-law of my household, I say, 'Though you are adorned with agates and corals, this does me no good. Have you no compassion for me? You have not asked a single lama to make some connection with me by dedicating your wealth on my behalf. Nothing would be of greater benefit for me than the cleansing ritual of Akshobhya, the deity in the southern gate of the mandala of Vairocana.'"

I recited the mani mantra, and for a short while he was at least able to rest. But, as before, he began experiencing his confused perceptions.

〰️ In addition, there were many lamas and monks in a fine-looking house made of iron. Although they seemed gentle enough at first, their minds suddenly became upset and they began shouting vile language all at once. In disbelief I approached them and saw flames issuing from their mouths, smoke pouring from their nostrils, and iron saws buzzing on the crowns of their heads. When I asked them what actions had led to this result, they replied that they had engaged in idle talk during rituals performed for the faithful (both living and dead), while associating with yogins who were completing formal deity practices, and while attending group rituals in their temples. They had interrupted others' meditations with their chatter, quarreled during feast offerings, and created a cacophonous din.

〰️ A wandering pilgrim appeared wearing torn and ragged garments and carrying a prayer flag on a stick.[21] Yama Dharmaraja manifested with his retinue and, showing his

delight, spoke as follows: "What great benefits and advantages there are to the Buddhadharma! And there is nothing
greater than the exalted dharma of a prayer flag. Prayer flags
are the root of the dharma. The mani mantra is the essence
of the dharma. The *siddhi* mantra brings liberation from the
narrow passage of the bardo.[22] The nyungnay fasting ritual is
the teacher showing the path to liberation. One hundred
thousand mani stones are the garland of the dharma.[23] The
act of saving lives is the chariot on the path. The casting of
satsas is the suppression of lower states of rebirth.[24] Going on
pilgrimages is the broom that sweeps away the effects of
harmful actions. Showing homage with prostrations uproots
faults. Tara is the outer source of refuge. Gathering the accumulations of merit and pristine awareness is the provision for
future lifetimes. Compassion is the central pivot of the
dharma. Therefore, my child, go happily to Potala."

The pilgrim passed by, leading about one thousand beings
connected to him through speech and touch.

Om mani padme hung hri.

ᢀ| The venerable Tara spoke to me:

Those who do not remove their hats when a lama comes into
    their presence,
once they have experienced the hells will take rebirth as
    bighorn sheep.
Those who do not rise and remain standing when monks
    come into their presence,
once they have experienced the hells will take rebirth as
    lame people.
Those who do not offer clean butter lamps will take rebirth
    in a pit of fire.
Those who step over or let their clothes cover the three
    representations of the Jewels[25]

will take rebirth as mutes or as unclean worms.
Those who spit or expel snot in temples
will take rebirth in the Hell of the Swamp of Rotting
    Corpses.
Those who eat meat from an animal killed the same day,
    without purifying it through confession,
will take rebirth as bloodthirsty demons.
Worthless sycophants who misappropriate the property of the
    Three Jewels
will take rebirth as pretas or their guardians in the preta
    realms.
Those who partake of unconsecrated alcohol
will take rebirth in the Crying Hell.
Those who make use of the seats of the ordained sangha
will take rebirth in the temporary hells.
Stripping vestments from the three kinds of symbolic
    representations,
carelessly misappropriating the property of the sangha,
and especially stealing communal property of the sangha,
robbing or beating yogins in solitary retreat—
these acts will lead to rebirth in the eight cold hells.
Those and others who gather karma by the power of anger
will take rebirth as hell beings;
by the power of avarice, as pretas;
and by the power of stupidity, as animals.
May those sentient beings who experience the three lower
    realms
be reborn on Potala Mountain.

Om mani padme hung hri.

ॐ॰॰| As well, there were many people of the Gyashod
clan. Gonpo Dargyay was chained, without hope of release,
in the middle of the six-arched bridge over the fordless
brown river of the dead. Smoke arose from his flesh as it
burned, and he suffered unimaginable pain. The minions of
the hells, with the heads of tigers and stags, were guarding

him. He said that recitation of the mani mantra would be a means to purify his suffering and faults, and that it would be of great benefit if others confessed his harmful actions on his behalf.

I asked Tara what actions had led to this result. She replied, "When this man was the ruler of his region, he did not distribute wealth and food or dispense justice properly, and he acted with ill-will."

The deer hunter Tsewang Gonpo was in the Reviving Hell. He said that he would be liberated if others carved in stone the *Sutra of Liberation*, which purifies the effects of harmful actions. I asked what actions had led to this result, and Tara replied, "The slaying of harmless deer."

Tashi Wangkhyug was suffering in the Black Thread Hell. He gave me a message to bring back: If a hundred million recitations each of the hundred-syllable mantra of Vajra-sattva, the mani mantra, and the siddhi mantra were performed on his behalf, he would attain a human rebirth.

Tsewang Gonpo was suffering on top of Shangma Mountain. He said that if a hundred or thousand nyungnay fasting rituals were practiced strenuously on his behalf, he would attain an excellent human rebirth.

Among the people of Gyashod, a number of those with virtuous minds—lamas, monks, and laypersons—were in pure realms, including the old monk Padma Kalzang, Tsering Dondrub, Dontse, as well as one called Barchhung Dragho, who said that he had been reborn in a pure realm out of the compassion of the venerable Drimed Khakyod Wangpo Rinpoche.

The majority of those from the Nat'har clan who had practiced dharma diligently had been reborn on Potala Mountain, while those without connection to holy persons, who had spent their lives engaging in harmful acts, were undergoing rebirth after rebirth in lower states. A monk named Hulay Buchhung was suffering in the bardo. One named Natar Alug Chhödzin had taken a fortunate rebirth. The monk Lodrö Zangpo was in Tara's pure realm of Yulokod.

Lhari Yontan, although he had practiced virtue and given up harmful acts, had entertained very serious wrong views and had been reborn in a realm where he was imprisoned in a house watched over by four denizens. When I asked Yontan whether I should request that virtue be practiced on his behalf in the human realm, the old monk replied that I should leave him to experience the effects of his actions until his karma was played out. He said that after suffering like this for three years, he would be reborn on Potala Mountain.

Kunzang and Tendzin Wanggyal had been reborn on Potala Mountain. Samyay Monlam of the Khamtay family was in this pure realm. He said, "I have a message for my youngest son. Tell him, 'Do not kill stags, wild sheep, or antelopes. Do not lead the life of a thief or a bandit. Do not tell lies or swear oaths. Do not steal from or fight with your older brothers. Practice what virtue you can with the mani mantra and the nyungnay fasting ritual!' "

A woman named Dronma had gone to Potala, supplicating many lamas. A tulku of the Natar commune named Adam was also on Potala Mountain. He said that although in order to benefit beings he had taken rebirth once in the Apal family of the lamas of the district of Nyagrong, owing to obstacles in that lifetime he had passed into nirvana.

Petsa Gonpo Rinchhen was also present; he said that he had been reborn in that pure realm through the compassion of Tromge Kundun Rinpoche.

༄༅། Eighty thousand leagues beyond this realm I came to a huge and fearsome cliff face of dark red rock, equal in height to the three-thousand-fold universe.[26] In the midst of myriad weapons, beside a terrible fortress of skulls, was the lord of death, Yama, sucking the life and breath out of the three realms of existence,[27] casting all mortal beings without exception onto the rack, holding the three planes of existence[28] in his belly. With his consuming maw gaping, his twitching tongue curled back, his sharp biting fangs bared, his hands reaching out to clutch, he was horrifying. He had a man's body with the head of a red bull, piercing horns of iron, and two staring eyes shining like the sun and the moon. Tongues of scorching fire shot from him. He had the speed and agility of the wind, and shook heaven and earth with his terrifying bellows of laughter. When I laid eyes on this fierce vision of unbridled wrath and heard his deafening roar, I felt as though I would faint.

Holding the southern continent[29] of this world of sorrow in his mouth (a mouth that seemed to encompass heaven and earth), he could make the world tremble with the sound of his tongue hitting his palate. Whereas once there had been a swirling ocean of dark red blood when he clamped his mouth shut, this year there were only a few drops of blood like dew. This was because Khakyod of the Tromge family, Dza Konchhog, and other holy individuals had passed away, and thus in that year many beings had not had to die.[30] Although many horrifying things happened to me, through my supplication to the venerable goddess I was able to take a firm stand without fear.

⌇ Gonpo Samdrub of Tangkya was in a hell realm. When I asked Tara what had led to this result, she replied, "When he was acting as chieftain, he embezzled goods, defying established custom."

Dorje Dondrub, the son of Zangli of the Sadu family, was

experiencing unimaginable suffering. There were many aristocrats from the region of Hor in far eastern Tibet. And there were many I did not recognize. As an incredible compassion arose in my mindstream, I recited the mani mantra to a melody.

ཨོཾ༑   As I, the girl Dawa Drolma, continued on my way, a yogin dressed in white, with long flowing locks of hair, approached, surrounded by a host of dakas and dakinis. He turned a prayer wheel with an elaborate brocade cover, and his feet did not touch the ground. He passed by me on his way to the plain of the hells.

When I asked him where he was going, he replied, "To the lower states of rebirth. I am going to lead away all those who have shared food with me. I am a master guide of beings, Togdan Pawo, whose very name means 'hero of spiritual realization.' " As he chanted the mani mantra three times to a melody, the houses of burning iron became palaces of crystal, and all the beings there were transformed into bodies of light. He headed off, taking them to the sublime pure realm of Potala Mountain, like a flock of birds startled by a stone from a sling.

The mother of all victorious ones, the venerable White Tara, folded both her hands at her heart and said:

> How wonderful—marvelous and holy guide!
> Sublime pilot leading all those connected to you:
> If there is no connection, you cannot lead.
> How disappointing for those who did not make a connection.

Om mani padme hung hri.

ཨོཾ༑   At the top of a *shalmali* tree,[31] black iron birds were plucking out the eyes of hell beings. At the base of the tree were fearsome women embracing the necks of these beings and then tearing their heads from their bodies. In my vision, these hell beings could not avoid going to them, thinking that beloved companions were calling out to them. When they fled, weapons fell on them. When they turned back, weapons sprang up at them, carving out their lungs, hearts, livers, and guts. When they ran uphill, weapons plunged down on them. Their flesh and bones were reduced to blood. Such is the danger facing lecherous lamas and worldly monks, nuns who abort their illegitimate offspring, and men who rape nuns or who, not content with their own wives, consort with other women.

There were those of lofty station whose names I dare not even mention, including many lamas and monks. One was Nyikho of the Sogru family, a monk of the Tromge clan who had broken his vows. Though he had been reborn once as a human being, after that he had taken rebirth in a hell realm through the power of his karma. At the base of a shalmali tree, heavily burdened by weapons, he suffered unbearable pain. The compassionate mother of all victorious ones (and I as well) chanted the six-syllable mantra three times to a melody. Freed from his load of iron, he left. If the recitation of the *Stainless Confession Tantra* and the *Sutra for the Confession of Failings* were commissioned from a large gathering with as much sponsorship and as many offerings as could be managed, and if noble prayers of dedication and aspiration were done on his behalf, he would be reborn on the Copper-Colored Mountain on the subcontinent of Chamara.

One called Atsul of this Sogru family, through the compassion of many excellent and holy persons, and by the mysterious path of truth that does not rely on cause and effect, had been born once in a human body. But after passing from that life, he had fallen into a hell realm. He was suffering at the base of the mountain of shalmali trees. Led about by an iron ring throttling his neck, his body was encased in garments of iron. Three fierce denizens with the heads of stags beat and stabbed and tore at him with lotus-handled razors until his flesh was stripped from his bones. He shrieked violently.

When I asked what actions had led to this, I was told that he had used false weights in his dealings with lamas and monks, spoken badly of members of the sangha, put on airs as though he were a master of religious dance, and so forth. This suffering was the inevitable result of these nonvirtuous actions. With compassion, I chanted the six syllables from afar.

The deceased man Atsul gave me the following message to bring back:

> I died at an early age, a young man ruined by death,
> ruined by separation from my parents and relations.
> I left behind my tent, herds, and possessions, so difficult to
>   give up.
> I suffer from the effects of my own harmful acts—they have
>   ripened for me alone.
> In order to free me from this unbearable pain,
> people can recite the mani mantra one hundred million
>   times,
> have the Kangyur[32] recited, and have the six-syllable mantra
> carved in stone tens of thousands of times.
> Then I will not suffer in this place, but will attain a human
>   body.
> Do not forget this message; take it to my relative Chhung
>   Lima.

༄༅། There appeared a lama named Yengmed Dorje, the intimate student of Padma Duddul, a lama of the district of Nyagrong. He came bearing a prayer wheel and a mala with a group of five of his students. He intoned:

Hri I supplicate the lama, the Supremely Compassionate
One.
I supplicate the chosen deity, the Supremely Compassionate
One.
I supplicate the daka, the Supremely Compassionate One.
I supplicate the protective deity, the Supremely
Compassionate One.
I supplicate the union of all these, the Supremely
Compassionate One.
I pray, lead all those sentient beings who have a positive or
negative connection to me to Potala Mountain.
Om mani padme hung hri.

Then he led about a thousand beings out of the eighteen
states of hell along a pathway of white light.

Ani Bumo, a nun from the region of Zurpa, also appeared
holding a prayer wheel and a yellow mala. She and a servant
called the mani mantra from afar to a very beautiful melody.
This nun led about a thousand people—ordained monks and
nuns, laymen and laywomen, beggars and blind people—who
were connected to her through speech or touch, along a
pathway of blue light to Tara's pure realm of Yulokod.

৩৩। Tsachhung, an old woman from the Tromge area,
was being crushed in the unbearable Crushing Hell. Her
screams resounded throughout the heavens. When I called
the mani mantra once to her from afar, a fearsome denizen
with horns on his head cried, "He, he! It will be difficult for
a single mani to be of benefit." When I asked what actions
had led to this result, I was told, "When she was in the ordinary human world, she stole goats and sheep and slaughtered
them."

She wanted to send word to her son, Chhöt'har, and her
daughter, Lukyid. Although at first I refused to carry any
messages for her, Tsachhung cried again and again, "You

must! You cannot fail to take my message back!" And so I promised to do so.

"Tell them this," she said. "Do not entertain hopes of becoming wealthy. Do not indulge in anger and hatred. Tell Lukyid not to vie with snakes in creating evil karma.[33] Carve the mani mantra onto stones. Request readings of the *Sutra of Liberation* and the *Stainless Confession Tantra*. Recite the mani mantra again and again. Dedicate the virtue in a noble way, and after enduring this for a thousand years or so I will be reborn in a god realm, still subject to the fall from that splendor."

So saying, she went on crying.

Om mani padme hung hri.

᠁᠁| Then, a middle-aged woman of the Lo family of Gyalrong approached. Driving about four thousand sheep before her, she plunged downward on a pathway of blood. The denizens of hell, such as Awa the Ox-Headed, Destiny the Monkey-Headed, and Raksha the Pig-Headed—an inconceivable number of minions of the lord of death—chased her, shouting, "Kill her, kill her! Beat her, beat her!" Trembling like a leaf, tears falling from her eyes, the old woman was led into the presence of Dharmaraja. Yama Dharmaraja blazed like fire in his anger, his whole face as black as coal, his eyes like swirling lakes of blood.

From his mouth came a terrifying bellow: "You, worldly old woman, so clever with your mouth, what kinds of actions have you committed, positive or negative? Don't hide or dissemble. Speak honestly!"

His stamping feet shook the ground like an earthquake. The denizens of hell clamored, "Speak quickly!" and stamped about together in a frenzy.

The woman went ashen, unable to guess what to say.

Beating her head on the ground, she tore at her chest with her hands. Among those present were the two small children of her karma, fair and dark.[34] The fair one seemed to have nothing to say; his face turned as black as coal. After a while, he spoke: "She once offered a horse to the estate of the Tsamtrul tulku of Dza, but when it came time to turn the horse over the old woman procrastinated."

The dark child danced and skipped about, saying:

Great evil woman, performer of bad actions in the ordinary
    human world,
great cannibal demoness who ordered the slaughter of beings,
cunning harpy—don't you recall other dark deeds?
There isn't a single misdeed you've contemplated that you
    haven't committed.
Whether this is true will be clear to the mind of Dharmaraja;
whether this is the case is known by his minions.
Take her away to a path without hope of liberation.

After the child spoke, a minion of Yama weighed the old woman's case on the balance of karma, and immediately the scales tipped end over end. Drawing a mark on the board of fate, Yama said, "Lead this one to the realm of the Crushing Hell. For many thousands of aeons she will find no release at all."

An army of the minions of the lord of death, shouting, "Kill her, kill her! Beat her, beat her! Ha, ha! He, he!" cast on her a rain of arrows, spears, and swords. Pressing her face into the dirt, they dragged her away.

Om mani padme hung hri.

One Wangchan, a petty chieftain in the Derge region, was the son of a rich and famous man, Drugdrag by name, and a woman named Tseyang Drolma. He was a very powerful chieftain who lived off the wealth and food of others; he was a harsh, aggressive man, without compassion. When the karmic forces perpetuating his life span were exhausted, he died and came to wander in the regions of the bardo.

Dharmaraja, as if suddenly laying his eyes on a hated enemy who had killed his own father, cried, "Swiftly, you minions of the lord of death, run, all of you! Waste no time in leading this evil Wangchan to me!"

Clamoring with cries of "Ki!" and "Ha!" they dragged him in. Those with hammers beat him; those with pincers plucked at him; those with saws hacked him; those with swords cut him; those with lances ran him through; those with axes chopped him. In the presence of Dharmaraja, the dark child told the following story:

> This evil man called Wangchan
> turned his back on the Three Jewels in thought and deed.
> He plucked out the eyes of fine lamas.
> He committed countless evil actions, cutting off the lips
>   and noses
> of many monks and nuns, laymen and laywomen.[35]
> He brought the weight of the law on many fully ordained
>   monks and imprisoned them.
> He caused famine that nearly killed the populace.
> He caused many thousands of sheep to be led to slaughter.
> He has a mass of nonvirtue the size of Mount Sumeru.
> What punishment he merits, Dharmaraja knows!

Immediately upon hearing this petition, Yama Dharmaraja, drawing a mark on his board of fate, said, "Let him be taken to the Reviving Hell and then to the rest of the eight hot hells, there to spend a period of ten thousand aeons without liberation."

The minions shouted, "Kill him! Beat him! Strike him!" Pressing his face into the dirt, they dragged him away.

Om mani padme hung hri.

၏၊ There was a young girl of the Derge region wearing a strand of agates, each agate the size of a house, strung on an iron chain around her neck. She was tormented by the weight and her pain at not being able to lift the stones. This was the result of having adorned her body with agates stolen from others, whether of high station or low.

Om mani padme hung hri.

၏၊ I continued on until I came upon a hunter called Tsering from the region of Kat'hog being led by four denizens with the heads of stags. Shaking like a leaf, he was dragged into the presence of Yama Dharmaraja. And oh, the two children of his karma disclosed all that he had done, virtuous and harmful, positive and negative.

The fair child spoke: "O Yama, precious Dharmaraja, this man could not feed, clothe, or shelter his large family. The old reprobate spent his entire life pursuing nonvirtue. Nevertheless, if you send him back for one more attempt and he practices virtue very purely, he will turn out to be one with nothing to be ashamed of and will return to your august presence as such." At this, the child wept.

The dark child presented the following petition:

He, he! This man killed the three kinds of birds—vultures, kites, and hawks—that soar in the sky.
He killed the three kinds of animals—antelope, deer, and wild sheep—that live in the mountains.
He killed the harmless marmots on the plains.
He killed the three kinds of animals—fish, otters, and frogs—that live in the water.
He trapped harmless animals in snares and nets.
He committed harmful and nonvirtuous acts.

From the mouth of Yama Dharmaraja came the following words:

Among harmful actions, there is nothing more serious than
    the taking of life.
In the case of this evil hunter
he had made a promise to the lama of the Getze clan not
    to kill,
but then committed extremely evil deeds beyond confessing.
Now let him be taken to the realm of the Howling Hell.
He will suffer pain without release for lifetime after lifetime.

Saying this, he drew a mark on his board of fate, and
pressing the hunter's face into the dirt, the minions dragged
him away.

༄༅། There were many more beings, the sight of whom my
eyes could not encompass, whose numbers my tongue could
not hope to tell of, whose thoughts my mind could not begin
to fathom. The evil ones were dragged down, while the virtuous were sent upward. All of this defies description; what I
have written down gives no more than the roughest idea.

In the presence of Dharmaraja was a woman known as
Bochhungma, from the region of the Dezhung family. When
the two children of her karma, the fair one and the dark,
were disclosing their petitions, the fair one said, "This
woman has some connection with Dzaga Chhogtrul Rinpoche. Her mind tends toward virtue."

Then the dark child spoke:

This woman served unclean food to learned lamas;
she killed calves by starving them to death;
she criticized lamas and ordained persons;
and so she has committed many harmful acts with her
    mouth, her hands, and her mind.

Dharmaraja replied, "Well, now, when the fair one was
speaking, it seemed that he spoke the truth. But while the
dark one was speaking, it seemed that *he* was telling the

truth. Weigh this on the balance of virtuous and harmful actions."

The monkey-headed minion weighed the woman's actions on the balance, whereupon her harmful actions tipped the balance end over end. Yama Dharmaraja said:

Each one thousand days among humans
is about a single day and night in the hell realms.
For twelve of these extended years you will endure suffering
by drinking boiling molten metal.
Then you will be led away by the power of the compassion
and aspirations of Dzaga Chhogtrul Rinpoche.

After he had spoken, the woman was dragged into an iron building.

Om mani padme hung hri.

༄༅། Next came Paltso, an old nomad woman with graying hair from the community of Nyingshul. She held a prayer wheel and a yellow mala, the beads of which she was telling. Chanting the mani mantra clearly to a melody, she came right up to Dharmaraja. Yama Dharmaraja, his face like the moon shining on snow, politely and delightedly said, "Paltso, having died and come to the bardo, aren't you tired? As to whatever virtuous or harmful acts you have committed, make a disclosure here in my presence."

The old woman Paltso made her petition:

I focused my mind on the Three Jewels as my only resort.
I bound up my will inextricably with the essential dharma.
My verbal utterances were the practice of virtue, and the
    circling of my mala was uninterrupted.
I established connections with people of excellent spiritual
    inclinations.
Most especially, I made a connection with Dzaga Chhogtrul
    by offering him a large piece of amber.

I made a connection with Adzom Drugpa[36] by offering him a
  belt clip.
Of those who tie a yellow sash around their bodies,[37]
there is not one with whom I, this woman, have not made
  some connection.
I poured out about twenty or thirty thousand butter lamps;
I recited aloud one hundred million mani mantras;
I dedicated all of this to sentient beings,
being an old woman of noble motivation.

With delight, the fair child made a similar petition. The
dark one had absolutely nothing to say. Now the mirror, the
written record, and the scale were the witnesses of the
woman's virtue and harmful actions. The minions cried,
"Look at these!" The lion-headed one peered into the mirror,
the monkey-headed one weighed her actions on the scale,
and the ox-headed one read the written record of her karma.
The three of them humbly submitted that all that she had
said was true, pleasing Dharmaraja immensely. He said:

If the common men and women of the ordinary human world
  were like this person, how much better it would be.
But even though they understand virtue and harmful actions,
  they fail to abandon some things and take up others.
They exert themselves in nonvirtuous and harmful actions—
  how ridden with afflictive emotions they are.
No one passes to another life without meeting me.
If there is dharma in them, I am the king of dharma,
but if there is not, I am the king of their harmful actions.
Now, old woman, you called Paltso!
Go, relying on this positive karma.
You will not fall back, so go to the pure Realm of Bliss.

After he had spoken, the old woman stood up and performed three prostrations. She said, "I will not go alone."[38]
Instead, she led some fifteen hundred beings that were con-

nected to her through speech and touch, passing slowly to
the Realm of Bliss in the western direction, murmuring the
mani mantra to a melody.

Om mani padme hung hri.

꩜ An old man, Dondrub, from the region of Gulog, an
iron cable piercing his heart, was being dragged along by
minions with the heads of tigers, leopards, black and brown
bears, foxes, and jackals. They tossed him up in the air, then
flung him down on the ground, calling out, "Ki, ki! Ho, ho!"
as they led him along. The man was wearing a shabby garment of marmot skins. When he found himself in the presence of Dharmaraja, his face turned ashen and he cried out,
"Ahhh!" After a short recitation of his virtuous and harmful
actions, Yama Dharmaraja said:

Evil, worldly person, slayer of marmots!
You have killed many thousands of marmots,
eaten their flesh and drank their blood,
worn their pelts as clothing—
you have made killing marmots your vocation.
In summer you killed marmots by pouring water down their
    burrows to chase them out;
in winter you dug for badgers, and killed hibernating
    marmots.
Such grievous negative actions are difficult to confess,
for what you have done is no different from killing a fully
    ordained monk.
You will have no chance for liberation for a thousand aeons.

"Now," he said, "take him away to the hot hells!" Pressing
the man's face into the dirt, the minions dragged him downward.

Om mani padme hung hri.

ༀ༅། Then there came about twelve fully ordained monks from the region of Sakya.[39] They were wearing the three monastic robes, carrying texts of the sacred Buddhadharma, and reciting aloud the siddhi and mani mantras. In the presence of Dharmaraja they made as if to prostrate as a group, but saying, "Please do not prostrate!" Dharmaraja himself stood respectfully upright. As his minions trembled in awe, the monks moved on, leading about twelve thousand beings to the Realm of Bliss in the western direction.

Next, a virtuous nun from the region of Minyag came in. Turning a prayer wheel in her hand and telling a mala of conch shell, she stood respectfully before Dharmaraja.

He inquired, "Who are you?"

She replied, "I am called Zangmo. I have amassed an ocean of virtue in gathering the two accumulations."[40] In a sweet voice she offered him the following song:

Om mani padme hung hri.
Lord in whose form all buddhas converge
and who is inseparable from Avalokiteshvara:
In the venerable presence of Sodnam Rinchhen
I make supplications: Grant me your blessings.
I have not committed a sesame seed's worth of harmful
   actions.
I am a religious woman who has attained some stability of
   mind.
To one with special compassion for beings in these spiritually
   degenerate times,
a lord of dharma who is an emanation of the bodhisattvas of
   the three families[41]—
to the venerable presence of Sodnam Rinchhen I offer my
   prayer.
Grant your blessings that our wishes may be spontaneously
   accomplished.

Grant your blessings that the sufferings of lower realms may
   be pacified.
Grant your blessings that we may enter the path to
   liberation.
Grant your blessings that we may be reborn in the Realm of
   Bliss.
Grant your blessings that the two kinds of benefit[42] may be
   spontaneously accomplished.
All those sentient beings who hear these words
need not suffer the pain of hell when they die;
they need not experience the confused apparitions of the
   bardo.
If they repeat these words every day without fail,
it is certain they will not go to hell when they die.
They will be reborn on the Copper-Colored Mountain of
   Glory.

Saying this, she chanted the mani mantra to a melody,
after which she continued on, leading about three thousand
beings connected to her through both positive and negative
karma[43] to the Copper-Colored Mountain of Glory.

ॐ Then Dharmaraja ordered two of his minions, Awa
the Ox-Headed and Destiny the Monkey-Headed, to bring in
Kunga Paldan, a fully ordained monk from the southern
province of Tsang. When he appeared before Dharmaraja,
his virtuous and harmful actions were disclosed. The fair
child submitted, "This monk has committed no harmful actions," and bowed his head in silence.
   The dark child responded: "This monk has broken his discipline and vows. He took vows in the presence of his abbot
and preceptors and wore the three monastic robes, yet he
was responsible for killing many people and horses. He
hurled invectives at those who were making contact with the

dharma. He is a morally bankrupt person who has thrown his samaya commitments into the river."

With this petition, Dharmaraja said, "Well, now! The stories told by these children, fair and dark, cannot both be true. Let us consult the mirror, the written record, and the balance."

Upon looking at these, the examiners respectfully submitted to Dharmaraja, "What the dark child declared is true."

Enraged, Dharmaraja shouted, "Take this morally corrupt person to the summit of the mountain of shalmali trees!"

The monk was led away by the minions, who shouted, "Kill him, kill him! Beat him, beat him!"

ༀ། A religious woman named Dronchhung from the region of Minyag was brought in. As her actions were disclosed in the presence of Dharmaraja, the fair child said, "This young woman, when she reached the age of twenty-one, shaved her head, took ordination as a nun, and set out on a pilgrimage to the area of Lhasa, constantly reciting the hundred-syllable mantra and the mani mantra."

The dark child made the following petition: "O precious Yama Dharmaraja, it is I who am qualified to tell this young woman's story. She is a demoness, a person of evil karma who has performed nonvirtuous and harmful acts. During her pilgrimage, she killed a number of creatures, and that is just an indication of the incalculable number of harmful actions she has committed, sir!"

With this, Dharmaraja said, "Let these petitions be weighed on the balance."

When they had been weighed, it was respectfully submitted to Yama Dharmaraja that they contained a mixture of good and bad actions. He said, "This woman must endure suffering in the Reviving Hell for one of the months of that realm; then, owing to the power of the aspirations she formulated during her pilgrimage, she will attain a pure human rebirth."

〰️〰️ A general of the Sa-ngon family, one called Sanggi Adzam from Jazi in the district of Nyagrong, had been reborn in the Crushing Hell and was enduring unfathomable agony there. He said to me, "My bride's name is Lumotso. You, girl, must at all cost relay my message to her. Tell her, 'You can benefit me by making a connection with some lamas; take my corals and body ornaments that you hid and dedicate them to the lamas on my behalf. The tears that you all have shed have become a rain of blood falling on me. Since I have a slight connection with the tulku of Jazi, ask for his consideration and help. Offer tea to the monks of Jazi Monastery and ask them to recite the mani and siddhi mantras during their group rituals for my sake.' "

So saying, he burst into tears. Although he faded from my sight, the sounds of his crying continued to haunt me. I offered prayers of dedication and aspiration for his sake, and recited the mani mantra for some time, but I had no connection with him and so no benefit came of this.

Om mani padme hung hri.

〰️〰️ A military commander from the district of Nyagrong Gangri, one Arta by name, was in the Black Thread Hell. Hundreds and thousands of black lines had been drawn on his body. With iron saws blazing with masses of flames, he was sliced along these lines from head to waist, whereupon the sides of his head were joined back together. He was then sliced from his belly downward, back and forth, with the pieces being split apart and joining again, so that he experienced these sufferings alternately.

When I asked the exalted compassionate goddess, "What actions led to this result?" she replied:

> This person led armies against many monasteries.
> He led people in destroying sacred tombs and monuments.
> He set fire to mountainsides, burning frogs and snakes and other creatures alive.
> He stirred up much social unrest, inciting internecine murders, litigations, and feuds.
> He was a chieftain who personally killed eighteen men and horses.
> It will be difficult for him to be liberated for a thousand aeons.
> May this person's evil karma and harmful actions be purified and may he be reborn in the Realm of Supreme Bliss.

Although she spoke in this way, he did not reap much benefit.

ༀ། Someone from Drured named Arkong was led into the presence of Dharmaraja while being beaten by minions with hammers, squeezed with pincers, and hacked at with weapons. Although both the fair child and the dark one spoke, it was of no benefit, for Dharmaraja became enraged, stamping his feet on the ground with mighty thumps and shouting, "Let him explain, and quickly!" But shivering violently, the fellow was unable to say anything.

The serpent-headed minion gazed into the mirror, saying, "This person held wrong views. He stated that there is no benefit to performing virtuous actions. He said that there is no fault in performing harmful actions. He claimed that the Three Jewels have no blessing. He said that as long as one is happy for the present, there is no need to concern oneself with the future. He delighted in theft, banditry, and oppression."

After weighing matters on the balance, the monkey-headed minion said, "If one were to heap together in one spot the bloody horns from the stags this person has killed, the medicinal musk from the deer he has killed, and the pelts and bones from the otters he has killed, there would be a small houseful. Here is a man who has denied himself the good fortune to pursue the Buddhadharma."

Then the ox-headed minion examined the fine print of the karmic record: "This person slaughtered animals during a holy month in which the effects of his deeds were magnified one hundred thousand times. Carrying a gun about, he slew many creatures—black bears and honey bears, foxes, lynx, and marmots. There is not one of these that this man did not kill."

Thereupon Yama Dharmaraja inscribed a mark on the board of fate. "Though the aeon may come to an end," he cried, "this man shall have no opportunity for escape. Send him to the Howling Hell!"

The minions, with fearsome shrieks, led him downward with his head hanging in shame.

Om mani padme hung hri.

ॐ Yama Dharmaraja spoke these words with his own lips:

You men and women of the ordinary human world!
Do not kill the fleas and lice that live on you.
Do not kill them, for it serves no purpose.
It is of no benefit to your food, not a mustard seed's worth.
It is of no benefit to the clothes on your back, being a grave,
    harmful act.
It will not do to kill them between your teeth and nails,
for that is no different from killing your own offspring.
If instead you free them and let them live, this will be of
    enormous benefit.

If you kill them, you need only look at what has happened to
those men down there to see what will be your fate.

There were many thousands of men experiencing the
agony of being crushed between two mountains. One called
Yardo from the T'hromt'hog family was there. The bodies of
some of these men burned with masses of fire; such was the
result of burning fleas in fire. Some were falling into water
and drowning; this was the result of casting fleas out into the
snow and sleet.

"Therefore," said Dharmaraja, "hold your hands still and
recite mani mantras."

Om mani padme hung hri.

ॐ༠།   Then Yama Dharmaraja said to me:

You men and women of the ordinary human world!
Only for the time being have you attained a human body.
Only for the time being have you been reborn on the Earth.
Only for the time being is the choice of where you are
    headed in the palm of your hand.

Make whatever offerings you are capable of to the Three
    Jewels above you.
You will not become poorer—in fact you will become richer
    in this lifetime,
and you will be reborn in future lifetimes with a body
    endowed with pleasure and opportunity.

Give generously to the beggars, blind people, and dogs
    beneath you.
Do not speak harsh words to them, for they are worthy of
    compassion.
Rather than fatten a hundred rich men for a year,
give a single handful of wheat or barley to a beggar.
Of these two virtuous acts, the latter is more special than
    the former.

Rich people who are comfortable, who have goods and land,
who are like the treasure guardians among the pretas with
    their food and drink, servants, and largesse,
squander their human existence, never having enough time
    and never gathering the accumulations.
They haven't even a moment to slow down and take a rest.
Although they have literally mountains of wealth,
    possessions, and food,
they cannot bring a single needle into my presence.

Family members do not listen to one another's opinions;
quarreling in the morning, they are fighting by nightfall like
    the demigods.
They will not remain in each other's company for long, but
    will go their separate ways.
So be good to one another within the family, and recite the
    six-syllable mantra.

People look angrily at their kind parents,
giving all the power instead to their spouses
and regarding the elderly men and women of the family as
    they would leprous corpses.
As people grow older they become faint of heart and sunken
    in spirit,
so treat them with respect, with gentle voices and soothing
    words.
For now, there is no more sublime form of spirituality than
    that.

You of the ordinary human world who repay the debt of
    kindness to your parents
are ready and able to go to the Realm of Supreme Bliss.
Those who make preparations, spread out seats, provide the
    necessities of life,
act as guides, and speak with gentle voices and soothing
    words
to those older people who come from far away on pilgrimage
are like those who entrust a wish-fulfilling gem to someone
    else.

They will have no difficulty in following the path to
   liberation.

Having faith in lamas and establishing connections with
   spiritual superiors—
this is like holding up a flaming torch in a darkened room
and will lead you to the Realm of Supreme Bliss without
   transition or change.

Having compassion for sentient beings and dedicating your
   virtue to others—
this is like a treasure house of gems that satisfy all needs and
   wants.
In all lifetimes hereafter you will encounter the wealth of the
   exalted ones.

The high king seated on his throne and the lowly beggar
   leaning on his staff—
for these two there is not a hair's worth of "high" and "low"
   in my presence,
so come to me having practiced the virtue of the dharma.
Don't you forget my message, Dudjom Drolma.
Benefit beings, both high and low, with this.

Om mani padme hung hri.

~~| In yet another fearsome place were many people who
had been thieves, brigands, and murderous hunters, who had
set snares for musk deer, cheated others in business, told lies
and blasphemed, who had robbed their helpless elders, spoken ill of or beaten monks, killed dogs, horses, and snakes—
an incalculable number of people who had engaged in the
ten kinds of nonvirtuous actions.[44]

Among them was a butcher named Atsog, who was led
sobbing into the presence of Dharmaraja. The minions ha-
rassed him, shouting fiercely, "Kill, kill him! Beat, beat him!"
Thereupon the ox-headed minion, Awa Langgo, said to him:

When you were in the ordinary human world,
you laughed aloud when committing the harmful acts that are
    the cause of this.
As a result you will cry out in misery as you experience a
    lower destiny.
What is the use of crying now, when you're on the plains of
    hell?

They clubbed him on the head with a hammer, sliced his
back with a saw, pierced his chest with a short spear, and
cast a hail of weapons on him. Having inquired into the virtuous and harmful actions that he had committed, they
dragged him to the Hell of Intense Heat.

Om mani padme hung hri.

꧅ One Chhungdron of the Gojo region, as well as
Paldron Dalo and her daughter, had administered poison to a
lama, seduced monks, and slandered their spiritual superiors.
The end result was that their backs were weighed down with
boulders of molten metal, their tongues were sliced with iron
swords burning with fire, and boiling molten metal was
poured into their mouths.

Tara said:

Harmful acts of the body are like a filthy swamp of
    quicksand:
It feels soft, yet because of it suffering arises.
Harmful acts of speech are like blazing tongues of fire:
Though a spark is small, it can burn up mountains of virtue.
Harmful acts of mind are like virulent poison:
Although sweet in the mouth, they bring great torment in
    lower realms.
For those who have performed harmful actions of body,
    speech, and mind,
may the effects be quelled like frost struck by the sun.

Om tare tam soha.

ᩀ᩠ᩀ   One called Argong from the region of Barong had persuaded the consort of a lama to run away with him, but they had died and were wandering in the land of Yama. I saw the lord of death, Yama Dharmaraja, inflict various punishments on them. Many flesh-eating creatures tore at their bodies; there was no limit to the pain they felt. Then came a lama dressed in white with his hair in flowing locks. He chanted the vajra guru mantra three times to a melody and moved on, leading the consort along a pathway of white light.

Om mani padme hung hri.

ᩀ᩠ᩀ   There were countless men, women, and children from the region of Barong. I have no time to record all their names, but if you wish to ask further and are sincerely concerned, I have much I could tell you, provided you have not broken samaya with me or been deceitful toward me in any way.

There were also about twelve poachers from the region of Dartsedo,[45] about whom the following was said:

> In their cruelty and anger they had laid traps of yak-hair felt.
> The blood of those they had killed swirled like a lake.
> The loot they had robbed and plundered was piled up like a
>   mountain.
> They dragged all connected to them to evil destinies.

Looking at the fine print, Awa the Ox-Headed said, "For the sake of the Gya Truglo family, these men spilled the blood of people with knives over two large regions. They are ringleaders responsible for the murder of many people. They have committed so many harmful actions that I cannot even mention all of them."

With terrible roars of "Kill, kill them! Beat, beat them!"

the minions of the lord of death led them all to the Hell of Intense Heat with their heads hanging down.

Om mani padme hung hri.

ৡ৶৹৷ There were some ten women from the region of Sangen who had manufactured poisons. Karma T'harkhyin, Tsewang Dargyay, Gonpo Srung, and others were chopping up the bodies of each of them, tearing out their tongues, and gouging out their eyeballs.

As well, those who had assassinated lamas and destroyed sacred remains were cast into a pit of fire. Terrible minions of the lord of death, wielding iron hammers the size of houses, scattered pieces of their flesh and bones with each bashing stroke. As they died again and again, only to experience unimaginable pain again and again, their screaming cries could have burst mountains and valleys asunder.

Everyone there cried out to me, "Dudjom Drolma, say a mani mantra for us!" For my part I felt an inconceivable compassion and chanted the mani mantra to a melody.

ৡ৶৹৷ I continued on until I came across four men, butchers from Gamdzed in the region of Hor. One was called Buchhung and another Büja; I was not certain of the names of the other two. As numerous minions with the heads of yaks took turns cutting their necks with blazing swords, they cried out to me that they were experiencing the result of having slaughtered harmless cattle. They were enduring the unbearable pain of dying and being revived over and over again.

With compassion, I chanted the mani mantra to a melody and supplicated the exalted and venerable goddess Tara, so that the four butchers were liberated from their suffering.

They said to me, "Please take us out of this place." I urged them onto a pathway of white light leading to Potala Mountain, and in a joyous mood they passed out of sight.

Om mani padme hung hri.

ॐॐ| Then the exalted and compassionate goddess spoke the following words:

Do not serve poison to wise lamas.
Do not steal the food of dharma practitioners engaged in
    intense practice.
Do not practice dharma tainted by negative actions.
Do not desecrate the symbolic receptacles of the body,
    speech, and mind of the victorious ones.
Always shun nonvirtuous acts and practice virtuous ones.

O laypeople and clergy, highborn and low, of the ordinary
    human world!
Don't let your hearts be bound by the chains of aloofness.
Guard the cause and effect of karma like your eyes.
Through the virtue of the dharma, whether bushels of it or
    just a handful,
it is certain that there is none other than a single destiny,
so without doubting whether this is true
supplicate the Three Jewels again and again.

Practice according to the instructions of your lamas;
adopt virtue and reject harmful acts.
There is no benefit in feeling regret at the time of your
    death.
O lamas and tulkus, monks and nuns, realized yogins,
tantric practitioners, shamans, scholars, chieftains,
government ministers, subjects, from young children on up:
Hold this message in the center of your hearts.

At the very best, cultivate a supreme confidence and be
    joyful at the time of your death.
If not that, be without fear and unashamed of yourselves.

At the very least, have no regret.
Don't make mistakes! Don't make mistakes! Practice virtue!
Om tare tam soha.

꿍｜ There were many thousands of blacksmiths from the ordinary human world. Their bodies were covered with heaps of coal as large as Mount Sumeru. They were incinerated in fires that burned without separating their flesh from their bones, and pounded with iron hammers the size of Mount Sumeru. Then they were seized with iron tongs and burned as before. Their burned bodies turned the color of iron; they were broken into pieces and worked in a forge. Then they were burned as before. Weapons so large they had to be carried on one's back were plunged into their bodies, and they were dragged away with chains of burning iron. Then they were burned as before, and on it went. It was so terrifying a vision as to make me faint.

I asked the minions, "What actions led to this end result?"

"Ha, ha!" they replied. "These people forged guns and other implements of destruction—knives and war axes, arrows and spears—which were used to slay many people and horses. These people repaired guns that did not shoot true, lengthening and straightening the barrels and sights, and tempered blades and so forth."

So saying, many thousands of minions inflicted pain ceaselessly on these blacksmiths.

Om mani padme hung hri.

꿍｜ There were people who had caused strife within monastic orders, misappropriated the property of temples and monasteries, or invested and traded with the offerings gathered by the sangha. I was not able to identify them all. In one direction there were many thousands of them. Burning embers, filth, and molten metal were being poured into their mouths.

They cried out, "Alas! How tormented we are! O Father, O Mother! How great is our pain! How difficult it is for us to be released from this agony and suffering! When we were in the human realm, we didn't think there could be as much suffering as this. But now we see how very dangerous it is to meddle with the property of the sangha. It would have been easier to swallow poison, for only a single death would have ensued. Misusing the property of sangha members is nothing like that, for it has given rise to such immeasurable suffering as this. Alas!"

I was told that even if they were liberated from this state they would be reborn as pretas with inner defiling obscurations.[46] Those who had caused strife and factioning within the sangha were experiencing the lowest Hell of Constant Torment without any interval having elapsed between their former lifetimes and these later ones.

Om mani padme hung hri.

꧁ I also saw lay *tantrikas*[47] who had acted irresponsibly, old sorcerers, and ordinary people who had pretended to be lamas, inconceivable numbers of them vomiting blood and experiencing unbearable bodily pain. I saw many carnivorous creatures devouring them and many denizens of hell hurling accusations of their misdeeds at them.

꧁ O renowned lamas of today, both ordained and lay, a humble girl such as I hardly dares to address you, yet I must implore you. In the hell realms are trials that you can see for yourselves. Shall we consider these? You lay tantrikas, with your long black hair and your white robes, your spouses and your children, are numerous nowadays. Supported by gods and demons and possessed of a few minor psychic powers, you fool others with your claims of having visions of gods and demons. If you have the ability to think about this, do it now. May it not cause you injury, and may your lives be long. Such is my petition.

༈ The following was a message from Yama Dharmaraja:

Venerable lamas, monks, and nuns in this world
rely on many gurus in a superficial way without examining
    them.
They do not guard their samaya commitments, and
so make them a weight that will drag them to the depths
    of hell.

In particular, the lama from whom one receives
    empowerments,
who shows one the path to spiritual maturation and freedom,
and who points out one's own true nature
is the essence of the one thousand buddhas of this fortunate
    aeon.

For those who upset or go against the word of their lama
or who cause dissension among those spiritual friends,
    brothers, and sisters
who have entered the same mandala[48] and the same lineage
    of teachings,
no amount of virtue will be of benefit.
Not only that, although those who have committed harmful
    acts against buddhas
can purify their karma through confession, the samaya
    breakers have no recourse.
Although those who have murdered many thousands of
    human beings and horses
have the means to confess their actions, the breakers of
    samaya have abandoned the objects of refuge to whom
    they might confess.

To go against the word of one's root lama is of greater harm
than to kill a human being every single day.
Even if the one thousand buddhas of this fortunate aeon
    were to appear,
any lifelines that they could extend to draw up those
    responsible for this great harm would be severed.

It is not simply that oneself alone falls;
all those connected to one by speech or touch, like herds of
    calves and sheep stampeding over a cliff,
will be turned upside down and fall into Vajra Hell.[49]

At that time, the earth of the ordinary world will tremble
and many holy people will pass away.
For a thousand aeons there will be no liberation from that
    state;
rather, for countless billions of great aeons beyond counting
they will experience all sufferings at once
with absolutely no way to bear this affliction.

Alas, lamas and tulkus, both lay and ordained, in the
    ordinary world!
Offer prayers again and again, remaining at all times
    inseparable
from the root lama, who is equal to the buddhas of the
    three times.[50]

Do not let your three faculties[51] be distracted.
Serve your lama in whatever way you can.
Offer the possessions you acquire as a pleasing mandala
    offering.
If you can accept your lama's orders
and surrender your body and life force in the service of the
    lama,
then even if you practice no other virtue, such as meditating
    on deities or reciting mantras,
there will be no need to meet me when you part from the
    cage of your body.
You will be ready to go to whatever pure realm you please.

Since this message openly reveals hidden and secret topics,
you need not be shy or embarrassed—proclaim it out loud to
    everyone.
If you wish to listen to the advice of Dharmaraja,
hold what I have said in your hearts.
Samaya!

༈ I continued on in the hells to a place where about
eighteen copper caldrons were turned mouth downward. I
wondered, "How is it that these amazing things are upside
down?"

Thereupon Awa the Ox-Headed turned the smallest of
them (so large that it would take a horse eighteen days to go
around its circumference) mouth upward, facing me. Inside
were many layers of blood. My heart burned as I quivered
with emotion.

He said, "The fact that they were face down this year
means that many lamas, in particular Tromge Khakyod, Dza
Konchhog, and others, have departed for the pure realms,
taking along all those connected to them. For them there
will be no sliding back into cyclic existence."

༈ On a pathway of rainbow light—white, yellow, red,
and green—the great mendicant T'hrulzhig, the lama Gyurmed Dorje from Tahor, approached with a retinue of many
students. He was singing the following song:

Om ah hung vajra guru padma siddhi hung.
I see no realm of hell, only that of the pinnacle pure realm,
    the basic space of phenomena.
I see no Yama Dharmaraja, only the dharmakaya
    Samantabhadra.
I see no hosts of wrathful minions, only the peaceful and
    wrathful deities of the mandalas.
I see no fair and dark children of karma, only the self-

appearing dynamic energy of transcendent knowledge
and skillful means.[52]
I see no laypeople, monks, or nuns, only the pure realm of
the entire vast range of cosmic purity.
I see no end results of virtuous and harmful acts, only the
dynamic energy of intrinsic awareness adorning the true
nature of reality.
I see no distinction between those with a connection or
those without,
only that all are connected implicitly in the basic space of
phenomena.
I see no higher and lower realms of being, only the pristine
purity of conditioned existence and of the state of peace.
Quickly, quickly, everyone—follow me!

As he sang this, a light from his heart shone like a moon-
beam. The very instant it flooded all the hell realms, the
sounds of misery and crying abruptly stopped. The denizens
of the hells stood staring wide-eyed, filled with apprehension.
Even Dharmaraja disappeared for a brief moment. The lama
passed on, leading some twelve thousand beings to the realm
of Potala, whether they had a connection to him or not.

I prostrated, made offerings, and reaffirmed my faith and
joy over and over again. The venerable Tara also folded her
hands together and said, "That lama's name is Akara, also
known as Tahor Gyurmed Dorje."

As well, there appeared a lama of the district of
Nyagrong, one Yeshe Dorje, his body shining with a radiance
that was difficult to withstand, surrounded by a retinue of
many dakas and dakinis. From his lips came the following
words:

I supplicate at the feet of the great accomplished saint of
Lhangdrag Cliff.[53]
I am Yeshe Dorje of uncontrived view,

Yeshe Dorje of unconfused meditation,
Yeshe Dorje of unmistaken conduct,
Yeshe Dorje of the unwavering goal.
From an early age, I followed after a great accomplished
    saint.
I have brought my life and my practice to their
    consummation.

All those who have a connection to me I have steered to
    the path of omniscience.
Now all those who have faith in Padma Duddul,
the great accomplished saint of the district of Nyagrong,
and in me, an old man,
should come with me to the subcontinent of Chamara,
to the Mountain of Glory.
Om ah hung vajra guru padma siddhi hung.

With this, light shone forth and flooded the eighteen realms of the hells.[54] Then the lama led some twenty thousand people, lamas, monks, and laypeople, even beggars and blind people, to the realm of the Copper-Colored Mountain of Glory on the subcontinent of Chamara.

I felt an unimaginable faith and joy. The venerable goddess prostrated three times, saying, "This lama's name is Jnanavajra,[55] otherwise known as the mendicant Yeshe Dorje. There is immeasurable benefit for beings in merely hearing his name."

੭੬੧   Among many men and women from the community of Satod was a man named Wanggyal carrying a bodhi seed mala the size of a mountain on his back.[56] Unable to lift it, he cried out in misery, as the minions of Yama Dharmaraja beat him.

I asked a minion with a tiger's head what action had led to this result. He replied, "This man beat a wandering pil-

grim, a realized yogin, on the road to Tsiwa and robbed him
forcibly of his mala and all his other possessions."

Om mani padme hung hri.

ॐॐॐ There was one called Ashey, clad in dark maroon
cloth, who had lived in the region of Gakhog. He had slandered many lamas and holy spiritual superiors, faked his
reading of scriptures, and taken fees for reciting the Kangyur
many times without ever performing these recitations.[57] His
tongue had been torn out of his mouth. On the tongue,
which was the size of Aji Meadow,[58] were buffaloes made of
iron with sharp horns. Attached to the horns were burning
iron ploughshares with which the buffaloes were ploughing
this "field." The man's pain was immeasurable. A minion
with the head of a monkey told him:

> The words of the Victorious One[59] are like a wish-fulfilling
>   gem:
> Do not take fees for them or sell them to others.
> The speech of the lama is like a crystal vase:
> Do not throw it into the filth and slime, but cherish it.
> The most excellent speech of the Buddha is like an ocean
>   of medicine:
> Do not sit on the shore and die of thirst.
> Faking the reading of texts is like pretending that brass is
>   gold,
> but it does not become gold, and you experience this kind
>   of pain.

While the minion spoke, the buffaloes ploughed again and
again.

ॐॐॐ There were about nine men from the region of Rag-
chab in the bardo. They were not aware that they had died,
and their minds were attached to their wealth and property

and to their parents. They and many others had no control over where they were going.

In addition, there were about a hundred monks from Nyitso. Some wore a garment of burning iron like a monk's shawl; some a garment of burning iron like a monk's cassock; some a garment of burning iron like a monk's vest. I was told that this was the end result of their having participated in feast offerings with impure samaya, pretending that it was pure without having confessed and purified themselves.

As well, there was a man with graying hair called Atsang from upper T'hrom. Many minions of Yama were pouring molten lead into his mouth. They said, "This is the end result of this fellow's having slyly eaten food offerings prepared in his own and other people's houses, so that his leftovers ended up in the mouths of the members of the ordained sangha."

> I supplicate the exalted Avalokiteshvara.
> I supplicate Avalokiteshvara to guide us along the path.
> I supplicate you to guide those mortal creatures
> who wander in the lower realms of hell to Potala Mountain.

Om mani padme hung.

∾ৡ৷ There was a grandfatherly old man of the family of Lama Tromge, wearing a loose, flowing black gown. In his right hand he turned a silver prayer wheel, while in his left he told a mala of acacia wood. His name was Tromge Sodnam Namgyal, and he was chanting the mani mantra aloud to a pleasant tune. The denizens of hell behaved with respect and faith toward him. A householder and an emanation of a bodhisattva, he moved on, leading many beings on the path to liberation.

Lama Jinpa Dondan of the Zur clan, behaving in the cra

ziest way, passed by, holding a mala of bone and chanting the
vajra guru mantra to a melody as he led many beings on the
path to liberation.

One Rinchhen of the Kyompa family, a patron of Tromge
Chhogtrul, was in the realm of the hells, chanting the mani
mantra to a melody in clear tones. Proclaiming, "Chhogtrul
Dorje Chang knows all!"[60] he led several people to the realm
of Potala Mountain.

〰️| Someone named Buchhung, from the region of Nyö-
shul, was in the Reviving Hell. He asked me to recite the
mani mantra for him, or even a single *Om.*

"Who are you?" I asked.

"I am your maternal uncle."

"Then how is it that you were not saved by Orgyan
T'hutob Lingpa?"

"My suffering," he said, "is the result of faults committed
during my conversations with that lama."

After I called the mani mantra to him from afar three
times, he passed on, vanishing from my sight and going I
knew not where.

Om mani padme hung hri.

〰️| A denizen of hell with an owl's head was leading
many people on a plain of burning iron, causing pain to
many, both lay and ordained. This owl-headed denizen said
to me, "Worldly girl with lofty manner, don't step on this
copper knife of mine."

I recited the mani mantra over and over again. "Please act
as an ally to these beings," I pleaded.

The denizen was incensed by my request. "What sort of
virtuous and harmful acts have you committed? Explain
yourself well!" he said.

"I have been everywhere, from the Copper-Colored Mountain of Glory on down and from the great plain of burning iron in the hells on up. I have set forth my virtuous and harmful actions, the positive and the negative, in the presence of Dharmaraja. I am a girl who lives by the cause and effect of karma. And what sort of virtuous and harmful acts have *you* committed?"

He said nothing but just stood there smiling.

Om mani padme hung hri.

༄༅། There was an old woman named Argong from the community of Barchhung. As the end result of having killed moles, she was being beaten and struck by a denizen with a mole's head. She gave me a message to bring back: If on her behalf one hundred million mani mantras, the *Stainless Confession Tantra,* the *Confession of Harmful Actions*, and the *Sutra of Liberation* were carved in stone and donations were made to many assemblies of monks, she would be reborn as a lay tantrika in the region of Derge.

As she said this, owing to the aspirations of a lama of the Ango clan of Barchhung she visited a pure realm briefly; but then that karma exhausted itself, and as the result of having killed a human being she was reborn in the Reviving Hell.

To relieve her of the iron collar ring that was choking her, I supplicated the supremely compassionate Avalokiteshvara and called out the mani mantra to her from afar, whereupon the ring was removed.

It seemed to me that she would attain a human birth in about seven lifetimes. She said that in order for her to be liberated people would have to perform confession and purification (specifically, one hundred million mani mantras, one hundred million siddhi mantras, one million three hundred thousand hundred-syllable mantras of Vajrasattva, and the

Confession of Harmful Actions); she could then be reborn in the pure realm of Avalokiteshvara once she had spent one lifetime as a human.

༄༅།   The tongue of one Nyima P'huntsog from the region of Tsang in south central Tibet was stretched to the size of an entire country. It was filled with iron spikes in all four directions, and onto it was poured boiling molten metal. This, I was told, was the end result of his having blasphemed and lied, and especially of his having had incorrect views concerning the members of the ordained sangha.

Someone named Dondrub, as the end result of having set houses on fire, was being held by denizens of hell over a great blazing fire of burning hot iron, scorched until his bones were still barely connected to one another. Finally, he was revived and went on suffering in this way.

Boiling molten metal was being poured into the mouth of Tsering Drolma, the consort of one Lama Tanpa of Minyag, as the result of her having poisoned the lama. Because of her intense suffering, tears poured from both her eyes like a year's rainfall. The denizens made frightful noises, a din like the thundering of a thousand dragons, enough to split heaven and earth asunder.

Seven men from the province of Golog, including Tsering the Slayer of Wild Yaks, were being hooked on the horns of many wild yaks made of iron, then hurled to the ground and gored. Molten metal was being poured into the mouths of their wives, Chhimed Dronma and the rest, so that from all their orifices red tongues of flame blazed forth. Their suffering was extreme.

Gonpo Dargyay Tsogo, Je Nyima, and others from Dartsedo, as the end result of having polluted the tea of assemblies of the ordained sangha and of having beaten or struck monks of the sangha, were struggling to cross the fordless river of the dead; their cries of intense suffering were clamorous.

༄༅། At that point, Yama Dharmaraja gave me the following message to bring back:

Take this message to the lamas:
In the ultimate view of the fundamental nature of reality free of elaboration,
one must be like space, without falling into any extremes.
In cultivating the stages of development and completion, the spontaneous presence of sheer lucidity,
one must be like a mountain, without any shifting or vacillation.
In the deportment of pristine awareness, the natural freedom of the five poisons,[61]
one must be like the ocean, without acceptance or rejection.
To act for the welfare of beings, leading the way in benefiting others,
one must be like a father or mother, without making judgments based on intimacy or distance.
To discover the goal that is the spontaneous accomplishment of the two kinds of benefit,
one must be like one who has gone to the Isle of Gold and not lost what one has obtained there.
Someone like that is extremely kind, the most sublime of those who care for the teachings and beings.

Those, on the other hand, who affect the manners of lamas,
who perform p'howa[62] for others without understanding their own minds,
who reduce the secret mantra[63] to the mumbling of empty rituals for the sake of food and wealth,
who proclaim themselves experts in benefiting others while being desirous of amassing wealth,

who merely imitate the sacred Buddhadharma without having
   freed their own mindstreams,
and who lead many people, both living and dead, on incorrect
   paths:
Let all who have behaved in these ways come into my
   presence!

And bear a message to the monks:
 Those who follow in the footsteps of the Teacher, the
   completely perfected Buddha,
who hold the trust of the sacred dharma of the sutras and
   tantras,
whose bodies are adorned with the victory banner of the
   saffron robes of complete purity,
and who have stopped all injurious behavior and brought
   together all virtue:
They are a field for the two accumulations[64] and are
   worshiped by the gods.
 Those who bear the marks of the children of the victorious
   ones yet destroy the teachings of the victorious ones,
whose impulses are directed toward worldly pursuits,
who indulge in women and wine as the essence of their
   spiritual practice,
who engage in the ten kinds of nonvirtuous action:
Let all who have acted in these ways come into my presence!

And bear a message to the dakini consorts:[65]
Those who first ripen their mindstreams with empowerment
   and maintain pure samaya,
who then become skilled in the key points of the stages of
   development and completion,
and are endowed with experience and practice,
and who finally reach the limits of accomplishment through
   the path of the four degrees of joy:[66]
Such people reside in the midst of those who hold intrinsic
   awareness.
But those who are selfish and are great deceivers with
   seductive ways,

who then choose the maras as their companions and cause
   conflict, suffering, and strife,
and who finally are brought to ruin by their adulterous desires
   and poisonous intrigues:
They will have no liberation.
Let them come with all haste into my presence!

And bear a message to the nuns:
Those who have offered the hair from the crowns of their
   heads to their abbots and preceptors,
who guard their bodies like wealth to be kept from thieves,
who regard their home countries as enemies and seek out
   solitary mountainsides and ravines,
and who pursue the practice of virtue with totally pure
   altruistic motivation:
They recognize their own minds and will have no regret at
   the hour of death.
In a state of joyful rapture they will go to whichever pure
   realm they wish.

But those false nuns who take ordination
but do not keep their commitments and flagrantly throw
   them away,
who finally hide their heads in the sand,
lusting after illicit sex and running around like stray dogs:
Let all those who behave in this way come into my presence!

And bear a message to the chieftains and rulers:
Take the Three Jewels as your principal source of support.
Hold to the kingdom of the dharma as your essential counsel.
Don't look to your own advantage, but protect the laws of
   virtue.
Encourage all to practice virtue, and prohibit hunting and
   fishing.
You will gain power, influence, and a noble body, and
   continually meet with the path to liberation.

But if you do not distinguish between the excellent and the
   harmful,

you will bring ruin upon your own faction and commit crimes
    against others
and spend your lives engaged entirely in internecine strife,
    contention, conflict, and quarrels.
For no purpose, you will bring many beings to grief.
Let all those who behave in this way come into my presence!

And bear a message to the men:
Those of you who, while at first committing a mixture of
    good and evil actions,
then establish connections with many lamas
and finally meet with the authentic sacred Buddhadharma,
arriving at confession as the antidote to harmful actions:
Go happily on a noble path that leads to more and more
    illuminated states.

But most of you behave nonvirtuously, as leaders of soldiers
    or bandits,
glutted with food and wealth, engaging in the five acts of
    immediate retribution,[67]
considering the lama and the Three Jewels to be a bane.
Your minds burn like fire, bent upon committing negative
    actions:
Let all who behave in this way come into my presence!

And bear a message to the women:
Those of you who have not betrayed your obligations to your
    kind parents
or been the cause of discord and domestic violence and
    contention,
but have served them and acted benevolently toward
    everyone,
shunning nonvirtue and pursuing virtue as much as possible:
Have no regrets at the time of your death, and go to higher
    realms of rebirth.

But some of you break the body and spirit of your kind
    parents,
being the cause of much discord and domestic violence and
    contention,

highly skilled in the use of subtle intrigues with strong poison,
with wrong opinions about everyone, slandering them again
    and again:
Let those who behave in this way come into my presence!

And bear a message to all worldly folk:
Having been born in a higher realm, turn your minds to the
    dharma.
Keep prayer wheels and malas in your hands without cease.
Pursue the recitation of the mani and siddhi mantras as the
    essence of your speech.
Those of you who have noble motivation and great
    compassion
will not meet me but will go to the pure Realm of Supreme
    Bliss.

But those of you who from the very first day of your birth
exert yourselves only in harmful and nonvirtuous actions
and turn your backs on the Three Jewels
will not meet me but will go to the Hell of Ceaseless
    Torment.

In this single dharma, developing pure view and compassion,
    taking refuge, and praying;
reciting mani, siddhi, and tare mantras and the words of the
    victorious buddhas;
preventing hunting and fishing, encouraging others in the
    practice of virtue;
ransoming beings' lives, using prayer flags, satsa molds, and
    prayer wheels;
performing nyungnay fasting rituals, prostrations,
    circumambulations, and the purification of obscurations—
there exist no greater virtuous actions than these in all the
    three realms.
Do not forget these messages, but relate them to everyone.

Then, on a pathway of white light, I saw people, both
ordained and lay, holding prayer wheels, telling malas, taking
part in fasting rituals, carving mani mantras in stones, string-

ing prayer flags, repairing paths and ledges, improving bad roads, encouraging others to practice virtue, casting satsa molds, lighting offering lamps, performing prostrations, going on pilgrimages, and ransoming the lives of beings destined to be killed. The countless billions of them were impressive of mien, joyful of mind, and happy in their thoughts. Reciting the mani, siddhi, and tare mantras in a low murmur, they moved on, going to the Realm of Bliss, Potala Mountain, and the Copper-Colored Mountain of Glory.

~~$| Such are my words, which do not violate the lama's directives. My kind parents and all the citizens of our region requested again and again that I relate my story, so I have here set down a rough account. May it please you.

In these degenerate times, when many great problems are proliferating, if we do not hold to the words of the victorious ones with conviction, what can be said for us? This dharma narrative of causes and effects that I have actually seen is untainted by lies; nor is it just a repetition of words that others have spoken. I have found the confidence to speak without distortion of these visions of hell that teach acceptance and rejection[68] by the grace of the venerable Tara and my kind lamas. If I have lied, saying that I saw something that I did not, or if, wishing honor and fame for myself, I have made pretentious claims about my spiritual status, may the flesh-eating *mamos*[69] swiftly rob me of my life force and breath.

For those who recite this, spread it, and practice according to it, engaging unerringly in acceptance and rejection of causes and effects, the exalted goddess will act as their guide along a path of rainbow light. If there are mistaken terms or names, faulty letters, forgotten messages, or secret words revealed herein, I confess these flaws in the presence of the

lama. I ask for the accomplishment of purity without obscurations in this and future lives.

> The soothing, uninterrupted flow of totally pure virtue
> through the hundreds of rays it radiates will banish the
>   darkness of accumulated flaws,
> bringing down a rain of benefit and happiness to all beings
>   equal to space:
> May everyone swiftly attain the state of the exalted goddess.

Thus, this account of how the girl Dawa Drolma spent
five days seeing visions of hell and other realms has been set
down in writing by the scribe just as it came from her mouth,
without any words added or left out and without error or
confusion as to the meaning.

> Good fortune, good fortune, good fortune!
> May this be a sixfold adornment of the world, blazing with
>   auspicious splendor.
> *Sarwa mangalam*—may everything be auspicious.

POTALA MOUNTAIN

THE PURE REALM OF
AVALOKITESHVARA

3

Homage to the Supremely Compassionate One,
Avalokiteshvara, great treasure of compassion.

᷈ Although this girl cannot speak as well as she
should, shall I relate to you a short account of Potala Mountain?

The realm known as Potala Mountain lies to the southeast of Bodh Gaya in India. The entire region is filled with beautiful flowers, and wish-fulfilling trees made of precious jewels grow there. Bubbling springs of nectar flow, and flocks of birds proclaim the dharma with their cries. Everyone is born from flowers, and there is no seasonal change from summer to winter. Not even the concept of suffering exists, while the experience of bliss and happiness is immeasurable.

Masculine and feminine bodhisattvas who have attained a stable level of realization enjoy sublime food of a hundred flavors, wear clothing of rainbow-colored cloth, and drink the nectar of the gods. They are free of birth, aging, illness, and death. They serve hosts of tathagatas[1] and listen to the dharma from the Supremely Compassionate One himself. Their mindstreams are freed through their immeasurable compassion. They bathe in pools filled with water of eight fine qualities.[2]

Here I found a beautiful celestial mansion, self-occurring and spontaneously formed, with walls made of five distinct layers.[3] Translucent within and without, supported by a thousand pillars of crystal and beautified by roof beams made of jewels, it was decorated with lattices of rainbow-colored light, as if illuminated by a thousand suns and moons. The wall beams were of turquoise, the coping of coral, the staircases of pearl. Circling this palace formed of five precious substances was a low shelf made of ruby, on which many thousands of offering goddesses danced playfully. Above was a vaulted roof of gold, with umbrellas of white silk and a wheel of dharma with deer kneeling and listening on either side.[4] On the four sides of the mansion were gargoyles with the heads of *makaras*,[5] strands of pearls hanging from their mouths with bells and tiny chimes that gave off delightful sounds.

The mansion's four sides were adorned with four doors. I entered by the western door and met a goddess of pristine awareness. Further inside, I perceived immeasurable wealth and sensory enjoyments, as though in a hallucination. Incalculable masses of offerings were laid out, surpassing even the wealth of the great gods of the Nirmanarati heaven.[6]

In the center of these, on a white lotus with a hundred thousand spreading petals, was the noble Avalokiteshvara, the supremely compassionate tamer of beings, with the freshness of a sixteen-year-old youth. His body was brilliant white, with one face and four hands. The first pair held a gem to his heart between folded palms, while the right hand of the second pair held a crystal mala and the left a white lily that bloomed next to his ear. My gaze was riveted on the major and minor marks of his perfect form.[7] He wore silks and ornaments of various jewels, with the skin of a *krishnasaranga*[8] antelope draped over his shoulder, covering his left breast. He sat with both legs crossed in the vajra posture,[9] his form shining with infinite rays of light. In my mind, he was no different from my own root lama, Drimed Khakyod Wangpo.

To the right of Avalokiteshvara sat his sublime son, Manidhara, Holder of the Gem; to his left his daughter, Vidyadhari, Holder of the Mantra of Awareness; behind him the lord protector, the buddha Amitabha; and in front of him his sublime consort, Shadakshari, Goddess of the Six-Syllable Mantra. His retinue was made up solely of spiritually superior ones who had attained exalted levels of realization, an inconceivable host of buddhas and bodhisattvas.

My companion Tara spoke:

This place is a land adorned with flowers.
This realm is a precious immeasurable mansion.
This deity is the deity of compassion of all victorious ones.
This retinue is a retinue of masculine and feminine
    bodhisattvas.
You, fortunate girl, should make prostrations and offerings
    with devotion.
Recite prayers of aspiration for a positive karmic connection.

I was filled with awe and joy, and began prostrating and supplicating, saying:

Compassionate Avalokiteshvara,
emanating rays of compassion in the ten directions,
I prostrate to you, inseparable from my sublime lama, and
    to your retinue.
I offer gatherings of unsurpassable offerings, real and
    imagined.
With heartfelt regret, I confess my harmful acts and
    infractions of vows,
and promise to avoid them in the future.
I rejoice in the inexhaustible power of virtue.
I supplicate you to remain forever, not passing into nirvana,

and to turn the wheel of the vast and profound dharma
    continually.[10]
I dedicate my gathered virtue so that all in the six classes of
    beings, equal to space,
may swiftly attain your state, O sublime and exalted one.
I beseech you, in all lifetimes grant me the most sublime
    blessing
never to be separate from you, Supremely Compassionate
    One.

When I had supplicated in this way from my heart, the
exalted Compassionate One's face lit up with a smile, and
I heard the following words, in measured and mellifluous
tones, the spontaneous and resounding vibration of his speech
that reached to the entire mandala of the retinue:

Om mani padme hung hri.
My lama is supreme compassion itself.
I myself am the deity spontaneously embodying the
    compassion of all victorious ones.
My enlightened activity extends to all beings, the objects of
    my compassion,
and in particular I care compassionately for all beings in
    distress.

You, my daughter, likewise of compassionate mind,
now have the good fortune of seeing me in this realm.
All those who prostrate to and worship me with faith and
    devotion
I will lead to my Realm of Bliss, through the force of my
    previous aspirations.

Through the power of my compassion, those in the six states
    of being, whose numbers are equal to space,
and especially all those in Tibet, the Land of Snows,
may make a connection to me by hearing my name and
    prostrating to me with faith,
and I will care for them with compassion, for I am known as
    Mahakarunika, Supreme Compassion.

Especially those who are defenseless, during the six watches
of the day and night[11]
I gaze upon them with compassion, my eye of pristine
awareness unimpeded.
I see them all and grant these humble people final refuge
from their pain,
for I am known as Avalokita, the One with Seeing Eyes.

Meditating on my form, recalling my name, reciting my
essence mantra,
and performing my fasting ritual—those who exert
themselves in these practices,
though they may have committed a heinous act leading to
immediate retribution upon their death,
I will lead them to the Realm of Bliss, for I am known as
Lokeshvara, Lord of the Universe.

Because of my former uncompromising aspiration to lead
effortlessly
all sentient beings who see me, hear me, think of me, or
touch me
to the ranks of Amitabha's audience in the Realm of Bliss,
the victorious ones have proclaimed me Khorwa Rangdrol,
Natural Freedom of the Cycle of Existence.

Alas! In these final days of the Victorious One's teachings,[12]
though I care for beings with more compassion than ever
before,
it is as though the rope from which hangs the hook of my
compassion has broken.
Owing to the tenacious power of nonvirtue, many are devoid
of faith and devotion.
It seems that they flee before my compassionate gaze.
Just as the sun's rays do not enter a cave facing north,
they are deprived of my presence, the manifest compassion
of all victorious ones.

While my compassion is without prejudice or bias,
through their habits of wrongheadedness, thoughts that are
by nature inappropriate,

beings wander again and again in the dark abyss of ignoble
paths and lower states of rebirth.
Seeing that their situation is self-made, that the fault lies
with themselves,
I find helpless ones in my care truly worthy of my
compassion.

The times grow worse as disease, weapons, and famine
torment them;
their life spans grow shorter as maras suddenly take them;
their speech degenerates as they become clever at deceitfully
beguiling others;
their nourishment degenerates as they engage in wrong
livelihoods;
their views degenerate as they plunge into the abyss of
eternalism and nihilism.[13]
Although the Victorious One's hand would stop them, they
are not stopped.
Certainly they suffer in their craving, do they not?
How worthy of compassion they are with their evil karma,
running after what they think is pleasurable.

Now you, O people of the Land of Snows, who burn your
own flesh,
since your suffering is arranged by you alone, ensured by you
alone, and torments you alone,
remember the great hidden flaw committed in the past, of
karma and afflictive emotions.
The time is ripe to give yourself some advice.

Only once in a very long while do you obtain this support for
freedom and opportunity.[14]
Now that you can meet with spiritual friends and practice
the sacred Buddhadharma,
and supportive circumstances have come together, spend the
rest of your life in just this way.

If at this time you were to plunge into the swamp of karma
and afflictive emotions,
you would perpetrate future suffering in lower states of
rebirth

where the opportunity even to hear the name of the Three
   Jewels is difficult to find.
The terrifying minions of Yama, lord of death, will come you
   know not when.
While your mind has this support,
take care to practice the essence of the sacred, divine
   dharma.

The Buddhadharma does not exist merely for appearance
   sake to protect you from fear and grant all your wishes;
it is not merely such hypocrisy, so look at your nonvirtuous
   mind.
Now that you have acquired a foundation of freedom within
   a virtuous realm,
you have obtained the seeds of unconfused moral judgment
   for gathering virtue.
Using three things—mindfulness, alertness, and
   heedfulness—the water and manure of virtue,
contemplate impermanence, which makes virtue grow.

Begin the cultivation of virtue with devotion and continuous
   effort.
Belief and faith are virtue's roots.
Compassionate altruism is virtue's trunk.
Bodhicitta of aspiration and involvement are virtue's
   heartwood.
The six perfections are virtue's branches and twigs.[15]
Intent, dedication of your own virtue, and rejoicing in that of
   others are virtue's leaves.
The four methods of influencing others positively are virtue's
   flowers.[16]
And emptiness and supreme compassion are virtue's fruits.
If the noble tree of virtue is cultivated in this way,
it will yield that which nurtures you and others, now and
   forever;
such is the infallibility of the interdependence of things.

Without the means to guard the noble tree of gathered
   virtues,
these are wasted again and again in the bardo.

Stupidly denying cause and effect, abandoning the dharma,
and impairing your spiritual discipline are a great frost that
   kills virtue.
Aggression, anger, enmity, and envy
are a violent hail that kills virtue's fruit.
Attachment to honor and gain and becoming ensnared again
   and again in the householder's life
are worms eating you from within, carrying off your roots of
   virtue.
Mocking or reviling lamas and bodhisattvas
out of overweening pride, arrogance, and haughtiness
is a fierce drought that spoils your gathered virtues.
The inevitable result of all this is a great increase of
   suffering;
it is a great enemy to the fortune of virtue you have amassed.

The antidotes to these are the three kinds of transcendent
   knowledge,[17]
continual reliance on four qualities,[18]
joy in the success of others,
profound reflection on impermanence, disgust with cyclic
   existence, and renunciation,
curbing arrogance, and training in an unbiased sacred
   outlook.
Be inseparable always from these guards and defenses.

Initially, be motivated by faith, devotion, and compassion.
Take the temporary precepts of the eight-branch vows.[19]
Focus your mind one-pointedly on abandoning the
   distractions of your three faculties.[20]
Whatever appears is the form of Avalokiteshvara, in whom
   all victorious ones unite;
audible sounds are the sound of the six-syllable essence
   mantra;
the absence of any ultimate conceptual framework is the
   uncontrived arena of bodhicitta.
Never be separate from these three key points;
continually recite aloud the six-syllable mantra—that alone
   is sufficient.

Gather together the virtue accumulated by you and others in
the three times,
and use it all as a cause for the swift attainment of
buddhahood by all beings,
following the example of the victorious ones and their heirs
with prayers of dedication and aspiration;
this unifying theme is like a bridle to guide a good horse.

If you continually strive at the four kinds of virtuous
practice,
at the moment of your death I will guide you in a state of
rapture
to the sublime pure Realm of Bliss.
Tell the people of Tibet that there is no doubt of this.

Do not hesitate! This is my affectionate and heartfelt advice.
Don't cling to this life; it is like a pleasant dream.
Don't be seduced by evil; there is no end to the harm you
can cause yourself.
Don't reinforce the eight worldly influences;[21] you will only
be fooling yourself.
Don't make all kinds of plans; remember that you might die
tomorrow.
Devote your threefold energy[22] assiduously to the sacred
dharma.
This is the greatest kindness that all the people of Tibet can
do themselves.

Should you have such a perfectly virtuous attitude,
continually recite the mani and tare mantras
and encourage all to practice virtue in any way you can.
Later you may go to whatever pure realm you wish.
You are inseparable from me, daughter, so rejoice.

Upon hearing these words, I experienced a sublime, joyful
faith, and to request the Compassionate One's blessing I recited the following verse:

Lord Avalokiteshvara, whatever your form,
and whatever your retinue, length of life, and pure realm,

and whatever your noble qualities,
may I and others become just like you.[23]

Folding my hands together, I asked that in the future we
might meet again and again. The noble one replied:

Those who maintain an attitude of devoted interest,
I am present before them;
I grant them empowerment and blessings.
Have no doubt of this, O woman of Tara.

I felt an even greater conviction in the truth of these
words and circumambulated the victorious one three times,
going around the inner courtyard of his palatial mansion, as I
recited the following verse:

In all lifetimes, may I never be separate from the lama, lord
   of exalted ones.
May I enjoy the splendor of the dharma,
perfecting the qualities of the paths and levels.
May I swiftly attain the state of Avalokiteshvara.[24]

༄༅། Here I shall make a few remarks based on scriptural
authority in order to lend credibility to what I have just re-
counted.

This exalted and sublime Avalokiteshvara naturally expresses the compassion of all the victorious ones. Long ago,
as many aeons ago as there are grains of sand in the bed of
the Ganges River, in this very world there came a great aeon
known as Graha. During that period, there was a universal
monarch named Aranemi, who sired one thousand sons. The
eldest son, named Animisha, gave rise for the first time to
the enlightening attitude of bodhicitta in the presence of the
tathagata Ratnagarbha.

Once, thinking with great compassion of all beings in the
six states of rebirth, in particular he vowed, "May those be-

ings who are without aid, stricken by suffering, caught in cause and effect immediately be free of suffering upon calling me to mind and reciting my name. May I never attain complete enlightenment until I have put an end to suffering."

When he had perfected his profound and extensive activity, he bore the name of Avalokiteshvara, a great and courageous bodhisattva. It was prophesied that in the future, in Sukhavati-padmapradesha,[25] as the regent of the sublime victorious one Amitabha, he would attain enlightenment as the tathagata Rashmisamudra-shrikutaraja and accomplish greater benefit for beings. In accordance with this prophetic vow, he acted even more strongly for the benefit of sentient beings of the six classes in general and the beings in the country of Tibet, the Land of Snows, in particular. As the *White Lotus Sutra of the Sacred Dharma* states:[26]

> The bodhisattva Akshayamati addressed the Victorious One, the completely perfected Buddha, the Blessed One, asking, "Blessed One, why is he called Avalokiteshvara?"
>
> The Blessed One replied: "Countless billions of sentient beings experiencing suffering will, merely by hearing the name of Avalokiteshvara, become completely free of their burdens of unbearable suffering. Whenever sentient beings are threatened by fire, water, poison, weapons, cannibals, harmdoing yaksha goblins, demons, imprisonment, thieves, bandits, and so forth, they will be saved. They will become free of the five poisons of the afflictive emotions and from all manner of harm. If they merely prostrate to him with total faith, all of their aims without exception will be spontaneously accomplished."

The *Exalted Sutra on the Array of Urns* states:[27]

> The bodhisattva Nivaranavishkambhin asked what the forceful radiance of the marvelous miraculous powers of the bodhisattva of supreme compassion was like.

From the mouth of the Tathagata came this reply: "The compassion of Avalokiteshvara brings beings in the hell realms to complete spiritual maturity. Having taken the form of a universal monarch dwelling entirely at ease in a pleasure grove in a city of pretas, he grants a soothing coolness to those tormented by fire and transforms all the pits of fire into lotus ponds.

"By scattering and dividing the guardians of the hells, he causes the lord of death, Dharmaraja, to prostrate to him and praise him again and again. He also cools the city of the pretas and pacifies the clouds of vajra hail.

"Guardians of treasure,[28] moreover, find their crude attitudes soothed and become endowed with bodhicitta. Ten great rivers flow from the ten fingers of his hands and forty great rivers from the ten toes of his feet. From the pores of this being who has a heart of supreme affection comes dew, which falls on the pretas. Merely by their tasting it, their throats relax, their bodies become whole and complete, and they are satisfied with the nourishment of the gods, food with a hundred flavors. The virtue of those practitioners of dharma dwelling on earth causes the pretas to rejoice greatly in the dharma and the sound of the Mahayana dharma to arise in their realm. At that point, the twenty lofty mountains of nihilistic views are smashed by the vajra of pristine awareness, whereupon these pretas are reborn in the Realm of Bliss, where they become bodhisattvas according to their wishes and are brought to maturity.

"In this way, each day he brings to complete spiritual maturity countless billions of sentient beings. Such is the confidence of Avalokiteshvara, which even tathagatas lack."

For the sake of those to be tamed, in accordance with their individual constitutions, capacities, and motivations, in the six watches of the day and night, Avalokiteshvara emanates as buddhas, bodhisattvas, *shravakas*, *pratyekabuddhas*, gods, celestial musicians, *yaksha* goblins, Ishvara, Maheshvara, universal monarchs, bloodthirsty demons, beings with sublime bodies, Brahmins, and Vajrapani, and teaches the dharma.[29]

Furthermore, calling his name even once is like calling the names of buddhas equal in number to the grains of sand in the bed of the Ganges River. Similarly, erecting a statue of Avalokiteshvara is equal to erecting images of all buddhas and bodhisattvas who have appeared, who are appearing, and who will appear in the three times. It is of greater merit to spend a single day meditating on the form of the noble Avalokiteshvara than to engage in the six perfections for one hundred years. These are some of the inconceivable qualities of the bodhisattva.

As for the benefits and advantages of reciting the *dharani*[30] of the eleven-faced form of Avalokiteshvara, it is said that one will eventually acquire complete mastery over four positive qualities: At the time of one's death, one will behold tathagatas; one will not take rebirth in inferior states of existence; one will not meet the hour of one's death unable to avoid its horrors; and having passed from this world at death, one will be reborn in the Realm of Bliss.

Through the six syllables of the mani mantra, all the sutras of the Buddhadharma are condensed; all illnesses, malevolent influences, and obstacles are dispelled; one attains innumerable positive qualities such as longevity and freedom from sickness; the sufferings of the six classes of beings are pacified; the six perfections are complete; and the kayas of the six victorious ones are achieved. In short, merely to see, hear, think of, or touch these six syllables plants a seed of enlightenment. All obscurations are quickly purified and lower states of rebirth are avoided. Passing through a series of noble rebirths in higher realms, one swiftly awakens to complete enlightenment.

By performing the fasting ritual of the Supremely Compassionate One just once, one eliminates forty thousand
aeons of wandering in cyclic existence and purifies all karma
and obscurations due to such actions as the five that entail
immediate retribution.[31] Perfecting all positive qualities of
the six perfections, one comes to dwell on the level of a
bodhisattva who will never fall back again. Women, too, who
perform this fasting ritual even once will, upon death, attain
rebirth as bodhisattvas of high levels of realization and turn
their backs on cyclic existence. One's physical involvement
in fasting purifies physical obscurations, and one will not be
reborn as a preta. Verbal restraint through the vow of silence
purifies verbal obscurations, and one will not be reborn as an
animal. The mental recitation of the dharani purifies mental
obscurations and shuts the door to rebirth in hell realms.
Thus, using these three methods of maintaining body,
speech, and mind in ongoing awareness, one is swiftly freed
from cyclic existence.

Serving practitioners hot cereal on the morning when
they break the fast of the ritual is equivalent to serving a
bodhisattva of the eighth level of realization; serving one
who has merely taken the temporary ordination is equivalent
to serving an *arhat*.[32]

One who sponsors such a fasting ritual will not be reborn
in the three lower realms of existence, but will be endowed
with the enlightening attitude of bodhicitta, come into an
inexhaustible fortune in all rebirths, perfect the quality of
generosity, and swiftly attain enlightenment.

In view of these and other inconceivable benefits and advantages, in the perfectly pure pursuit of virtue, rejoice and
exert yourselves day and night without distraction, motivated
by intense and unhesitating altruism, faith, and devotion.

If you live the remainder of your days meaningfully, you

will ensure your own welfare and that of others. This fact is borne out by the true speech of the victorious ones, the experience of all great spiritual superiors, and the direct proof of one's own intrinsic awareness, and merits your pursuit with devoted intent.

Without making a false start, you will become free from fear of rebirth and death; if not that, you will gain the confidence to meet death cheerfully; at the very least, you will die without fear or regret.

I fold my hands and pray from my heart that all of you will be able to do this. Again and again, I urge you to free your minds of indecision and remain honest in this meaningful endeavor.

Good fortune, good fortune, good fortune!

YULOKOD

THE PURE REALM
OF TARA

4

Prostrations to Avalokiteshvara.

Bowing at the lotus feet of the one
who looks on living beings with compassionate eyes,
I will praise this extraordinary deity
in order to perfect the two accumulations.[1]

Prostrations to you, Tara, deity among deities,
source of all spiritual accomplishments without exception.
Like a precious and wish-fulfilling gem,
you grant the fruition of all we desire.

Those sentient beings who wish to actually see
the pure realm of Tara in their minds
will rejoice in the cooling rays of pure vision
in the soothing shelter of the blooming lotus of faith.

〰️ When I was returning from Potala Mountain,[2] I soared up to the left, and with White Tara as my guide I came to a place where the entire country was verdant wherever I looked, beautiful and vividly clear, a marvelous environment with many extraordinary features. Pavilions of five-colored rainbow light hovered in the sky. Many kinds of flowers and lotuses grew everywhere. Here there was no concept of summer or winter. The wish-granting trees were in full leaf, and from them hung small chimes and bells. When the wind stirred these, they sounded the words of the Buddhadharma in the Sanskrit language, such as *Namo arya tare mam*.[3] Birds that were emanations of the Noble Lady—sparrows, ducks, peacocks, cranes, parrots, grouse, cuckoos, and swans—played everywhere. The land was filled with wealth and prosperity on an inconceivable scale. The mountains themselves consisted of gold, silver, turquoise, and precious gems. Everywhere were pools of nectar endowed with eight fine qualities[4] and elegantly appointed bathhouses made of precious jewels.

In this realm, there were no concepts of birth, aging, illness, or death. All the inhabitants were born miraculously from the hearts of lotuses. In no future lifetime would they hear an unpleasant or discordant sound. Those dwelling there were masculine and feminine bodhisattvas who had attained high levels of realization. This place surpassed the limits of the imagination; its size could not be measured. It contained thousands of immeasurable mansions fashioned of the five precious substances.[5]

In an instant, I had arrived at the gateway of the central palace—a vast celestial mansion of magical and marvelous appearance, having the power to liberate beings in four ways.[6] The very moment I entered it, I awoke from the deep sleep of ordinary rational consciousness and was free of the veils of ignorance. The inner vision of my pristine awareness expanded, and I experienced a surge of love and compassion.

As I passed through the western door, I met Guhyadevi, the Goddess of Secrets, who seemed extremely delighted to see me. Passing on, I came to a courtyard in which many thousands of goddesses, dressed in green, chanted the praises to the twenty-one forms of Tara in the Sanskrit tongue. Occasionally, they played small finger cymbals, golden hand drums, and drums made of sandalwood, ebony, "serpent's heart" wood,[7] and four kinds of heartwood, as well as cymbals, gongs, and flutes. They frequently punctuated their chant with music performed on this inconceivable variety of instruments. Upon hearing them, I felt an unimaginable sense of devotion; I made offerings in my mind and fervently recited the praises to the twenty-one forms of Tara.

༄༅། I entered a small house, where I found a goddess. She seemed very old, her white hair twisted up like a conch shell, but her teeth were in even rows with no gaps, and her complexion was as lustrous as that of a young woman in her prime. This exceptionally noble goddess sat with a large retinue surrounding her. She bore the secret name Gauri Girtima, but she was widely known by her real name, Ayurdevi, the Goddess of Longevity.[8] I performed prostrations and circumambulations, mandala offerings and seven-branch prayers, and prayers of supplication and aspiration.

She said, "What is this, my girl? How fortunate you are to have come into my presence. How marvelous! What karmic connection accounts for your showing up here? I am a heroine whose qualities are hidden. Graced by that marvelous deity, the venerable Tara, I have mastery over immortal vajra life."

She placed her hands on my head and showed great delight in me, reciting:

Prostrations to the one who has the luster of a ruby,
in the full bloom of the youth of the sixteen joys.[9]
Victorious in battle over the discordant forces of maras,
she bestows the accomplishment of immortal life.

She added, "Not even a representation of my image is to be found in either India or Tibet. Although an immeasurable number of yogis and yoginis, graced by Tara, visit this realm in actuality, in visions, and in dreams, not one of them has received an audience with me." I was delighted by her words.

ॐ। I continued on to the central immeasurable mansion. Inside, I saw that the five-layered walls were made of conch shell, gold, coral, emerald, and sapphire, all with friezes of ruby. The pillars and columns were made of red pearl, the main roof beams of quartz crystal, and the rafters of gems that grant all one's desires. There were wide windows and skylights everywhere to illuminate the interior. Atop a cornice of gold was a pediment of coral, supporting a bluish green vault of turquoise. In the four directions were gargoyles with the heads of makaras; hanging from their mouths were strands and loops of white, yellow, red, and green pearls, with tiny golden chimes giving off lovely sounds. Melodious music that can take away the suffering of those in lower realms resounded. The fragrant scent of the incense of the immeasurable attitudes wafted about.[10] There were fine displays of unimaginably lovely offerings.

In the center of the mansion, on a many-colored lotus with a thousand petals and a moon disk seat, was the only refuge, the very embodiment of compassion, the sublime mother of all victorious ones of the three times, the sister of the bodhisattvas, she whom both those in the human world and those in the heavens worship with the crowns of their heads touched to the soles of her feet—the goddess who sprang from the tears of the Exalted One,[11] the noble Tara herself.

Her body was bluish green, more intensely luminous than a mountain of turquoise lit by a thousand suns. Infinite rays of light shone from her form, which was adorned with major and minor marks of perfection. Her body was that of a youthful maiden sixteen years of age, clad in garments made from the silk of the gods and adorned with immeasurably valuable ornaments of precious wish-fulfilling gems. Her hair was shiny jet black, half of her tresses bound up in a topknot and half flowing down and covering her shoulders, interlaced with ribbons of blue-green silk that fluttered in the breeze. With her left hand in the gesture symbolizing the Three Jewels,[12] she held the stem of a green lily, the petals of which bloomed next to her ear. With her right hand held in the gesture of granting refuge,[13] she sheltered beings from the limitless fears of this confused world of cyclic existence. Her two legs were half-crossed in the posture of a feminine bodhisattva.

Many noble feminine bodhisattvas were circumambulating her in a counterclockwise direction. The adept Suryagupta was to her right, the bodhisattva Dawa Gyaltsan behind her, the poet Chandragomin to her left, and the lord Dipamkara in front of her.[14] Altogether, there were many thousands of principal figures with their retinues and an inconceivable host of hundreds of thousands of forms of Tara, including Tara of the Thunderous Dragon's Roar, Tara of Supreme Power, Tara of Spontaneous Accomplishment, Tara of Fearlessness, Tara of Rays of Light, Tara Who Tames Beings, Tara of Zang-yun,[15] Tara of Inconceivability, Tara Skillful in Means, Tara of Enlightenment, Tara of Central Tibet, and Tara of China. These were distinctly visible to me, but their bodies were not inherently existent aggregates of flesh and blood. Instead, they were illusory forms of pristine awareness, a magical display manifesting in myriad ways. I saw them in all their scintillating brilliance, like the stars and planets reflected in the vast ocean.

At this point, my grasping at ordinary reality spontaneously ceased. For a short time I experienced an inexpressible,

unimaginable sense of infinite cosmic order, a vast and totally unimpeded panorama of purity with nothing to grasp at
as ultimately real. I prostrated over and over again in a state
of faith and sheer joy. Approaching the venerable goddess, I
offered mandalas of the universe and seven-branch prayers.
With intense yearning, I prayed to the three deities who
watch over the Land of Snows.[16] Placing her feet on the
crown of my head, I sang this song in plaintive tones:

> Alas, alas, compassionate mother of victorious ones!
> Your beloved daughter wanders in the wilderness of cyclic
>   existence,
> set upon by the thieves and bandits of eighty thousand
>   thought patterns.
> She is on the point of losing her finest wealth of perfect
>   virtue.
> Seize her with your compassion, noble lady Tara.
>
> Now, as the signs of these degenerate times rage about us,
> the Victorious One's teachings are a sun moving toward the
>   abode of the water god.[17]
> The hosts of spiritual friends who hold the teachings have
>   departed to a realm of peace.
> The teachings of sutra and tantra are eclipsed by clouds of
>   sectarian prejudice.
> Seize us with your compassion, noble lady Tara.
>
> The many sentient creatures are without a place of rest.
> Constantly pained by the illness of karma and afflictive
>   emotions,
> they suffer the consequences of unbearable misery and pain.
> It will be a long time before they reach the land of
>   omniscience and liberation.
> Seize them with your compassion, noble lady Tara.
>
> The colors of the spirits of evil stand out in the sky.
> The radiance fades from the victory banner of those who
>   practice dharma.

Now that the world is filled with spiritual charlatans,
lest living beings be dragged onto perverted paths
seize them with your compassion, noble lady Tara.

The hordes of barbarians and border tribes bring the
    teachings to an end.
Battles are waged incessantly with the five forces of evil.[18]
The destructive armies of the maras are on the point of
    invading.
If you do not shelter us from these, to whom will you show
    your wisdom and power?
Seize us with your compassion, noble lady Tara.

I uttered many other prayers, my mind filled with longing.
The exalted goddess, placing her right hand, clearly marked
with the excellent sign of a wish-fulfilling wheel,[19] on my
head, replied:

Listen, O lovely maiden, Chandra Tara.[20]
In the past, in the earliest of the earliest aeons,
when I gave rise to excellent bodhicitta,
there was no one who aspired to perfect buddhahood in a
    woman's body.
Therefore, I conceived the following aspiration:

"I will appear in the forms of women.
I will bring this ocean of beings to supreme enlightenment.
The moment they recall even my name,
they will be reassured in the face of the eight kinds of fear[21]
and the pit of cyclic existence will be dredged from its
    depths.
Until I have brought them to perfect buddhahood,
may I never come to buddhahood myself."

With these and a hundred thousand other aspirations,
I made my promises and commitments.
And in this realm, while primordially a buddha,
I nevertheless showed the manner of perfecting buddhahood.
For all beings my compassion is great;

especially for the subjects of Tibet my activity is swift.
Therefore, wise and fortunate ones,
closely guard this command of the exalted goddess as follows:

In times of the five degenerations,[22] when only traces of the
    teachings remain,
when barbarian invasions will soon bring all to an end,
this noble support,[23] endowed with leisure to practice, is
    threatened by impermanence's toll.
If you are confused about cause and effect, consult the sutras
    and tantras to bring about happiness and eliminate pain.[24]
Wealth and property, friends and relations, father and
    mother are no refuge.
What will provide refuge? The infallible Three Jewels.

Especially, again and again in the six watches of the day and
    night,
pray to the three deities sheltering the Land of Snows.
Amitabha in the Realm of Bliss,
the exalted Avalokiteshvara in the realm of Potala,
Guru T'hod T'hreng Tzal in the subcontinent of Chamara,
the exalted Tara in the realm of Yulokod,
and the root gurus who are the essence of the unity of all
    these—
identical in essential nature, distinct merely in appearance,
without sundering or division, they are in a primordial state
    of equality with your own intrinsic awareness,
beyond union in the ordinary sense of coming together and
    falling apart.

Always direct your attention to virtue.
Do not squander this human life in distraction,
or pay mere lip service to the dharma,
but sincerely from the depths of your heart,
rely on faith, pure view, compassion, bodhicitta,
exertion, wisdom, mindfulness, alertness, and self-control.
If the three phases of preparation, main practice, and
    conclusion are complete, the fruit of your goal will ripen.

Especially, if the essence mantras of the three deities of great
  compassion—
the mani, siddhi, and tare mantras—
or even a single nyungnay fasting ritual performed by yourself
  or others
will remove the effects of forty thousand aeons of harmful
  actions and breaches of your vows,
what need is there to speak of benefits and advantages of
  regular practice?

Therefore, behave morally, without confusing cause and
  effect.
Certainly, you fortunate ones who are able to pray
will have no hardship or fatigue in coming
to the realm of Yulokod without hesitation after death.
I swear that I will come to greet you.
My emanations, as ordinary spiritual friends,
men and women, animals and birds, and the like,
take whatever forms will guide and care for others.
Since there are countless numbers of them,
have faith and pure view, and make supplications and
  aspirations.

Her words inspired immeasurable faith and joy within me,
and I prayed over and over to receive the four empowerments.[25] And though I felt the pain of separation from Tara
to be more agonizing than that of gods falling from their happiness, Tara said to me, "Do not grieve in your heart! We
will never be separate in any lifetime. I give you the name
Rigdzin Drolma, Tara Who Holds Intrinsic Awareness. Furthermore, a goddess, an emanation of the energy of my activity, will be with you constantly during the six watches of the
day and night, like one person talking to another."

ༀ། Continuing on, I came to a small room, where I met
the repa Dampa Gyagar, robust of body, his hair white and

thinning slightly. He had four sons and four daughters. The youngest daughter, named Chhang Trama, said to me, "It is good that you have come seeking me," and began a delightful dance and song to Tara. She was very affectionate toward me. Her father sat nearby, holding a longevity vase, laughing to himself. When I asked him to say a prayer for me, he laughed again and stared fixedly, focusing his attention for a moment.

I left the mansion by the western door. I bathed in a pond and drank of the nectar of immortal life. (If I had to record all that I saw and all those whom I met there, it would certainly fill many volumes, but I am unable to write it all down.)

〰️| In a place not far away I came across a *karandatava* tree, with roots made of gold, a trunk of silver, branches of sapphire, leaves of amber, flowers of ruby, and fruit of diamonds. It was a wish-granting tree and it seemed to cover the earth. From it hung silk banners of many colors, and strings and loops of pearls with small tinkling golden chimes attached. Atop this tree was perched the king of birds—a *masar* bird, though it was called by a different name, *karantava*. Its body was formed of seven kinds of precious jewels, and on the crown of its head was a crest made of a *sarvaphala* gem. Its plumage was more beautiful than a peacock's, and its cry was in Sanskrit: *Sarva buddhaye eka potala yana duhkhashantim siddhiphala hoh*, which might be rendered, "To attain nothing less than buddhahood, which is perfect in every way, go to the realm of Potala. May beings in the six states of cyclic existence be free of suffering and may excellent spiritual accomplishments be granted."

Sitting at the foot of this tree was an old white-haired man holding an ax called Arthachandra, Moon That Fulfills

Goals. As I rested there and partook of the tree's fruit, the man said aloud, "The boy sent by the noble Avalokiteshvara, Karmasarvamangala by name, sprang from the root of the karandatava."

At this, flocks of birds began calling out stridently, "Alas!" They flapped their wings, as tears fell from their eyes. Their king cried:

> Do not cut down the karandatava tree!
> The karantava bird will fall to earth.
> O man, may you live long and free of illness.
> I, the bird, will go to Potala.

I saw alternating scenes of the man cutting down the tree and the bird falling. I had many such cryptic visions. Then a lay practitioner, blessed by the exalted Avalokiteshvara, appeared and watched me while I recited the praises to the twenty-one forms of Tara. After a while he said, "These are the benefits of such recitation":

> All those who hold this prayer of praise in their minds
> will uproot all faults and failings without exception,
> increase positive qualities like the waxing moon,
> and be blessed by a thousand buddhas.
> O marvelous is this highest of praises;
> by merely calling it once to mind
> one will definitely be reborn
> in the most excellent sacred Realm of Bliss.

He also described the mundane and transcendent benefits as they are explained in the traditional sources.

༄༅། Then there appeared one who in previous lifetimes had had a samaya connection with Vajradhara and Guru Padmasambhava, and who was a guardian of hidden treasure teachings of the vast and profound Buddhadharma. She had later been the spiritual consort of Mila Zhadpa Dorje (the single ornament of the practicing lineage in the Land of Snows) when he was in the region of Mount Everest and Chhubar, and so had drawn his subtle energy and consciousness into his central channel.[26] Finally, she had been the personal guardian deity of the sublime tulku Jigmed Do-ngag Tandzin (a vajra holder of intrinsic awareness) and Dechhen Dorje[27] (a crown jewel among hundreds of spiritual adepts), dispelling obstacles to their longevity and directing the increase of their activities to benefit beings impartially. Known widely by the name of Tashi Tseringma, queen of the goddesses of medicine, she called out three times from the meditation center of my precious teacher, saying, "You, girl— Dawa Drolma! Come back to the human realm!"

When I heard her clear voice resounding, I began to think of my precious uncle, my companions and relatives, and my parents back in the region of T'hrom. My mind was filled with a special longing and I thought of going back. And so, with White Tara accompanying me, I returned in an instant. Five full days (that is, ten twelve-hour periods of day or night) had passed in the human realm. When my consciousness reentered my physical body, I sneezed violently. At first, I experienced total disorientation, as though I had just awakened from sleep, but soon I was filled with faith and joy at the visions of the pure realms and horror at the karmic visions of the hells.[28]

Uncle Trungpa[29] stood in front of me, holding a beribboned longevity arrow and looking at me fixedly with bloodshot eyes. I was unable to say a word, as though I were a bit shy. I was ritually cleansed with the medicinal rain of the seers[30] and with water used during the meditation practice of the protective goddess Vijaya.

Everyone was crying and excited, saying things like, "Wasn't it difficult? You must be hungry! You must be thirsty!" They were almost pouring food and drink over my head in their eagerness. Although I protested, "I feel absolutely no discomfort from hunger or thirst," they didn't believe me and insisted, "Eat! Drink!" They all felt joy as immeasurable as that of a she-camel on finding her lost calf, and partook of a celebratory feast.

I then rested for a day or two, whereupon my accounts of the pure realms of Potala and Yulokod and the hell realms were written down without fabrication or interpolation by Gyazur Tulku.

> The secret form, speech, and mind of all limitless victorious
> ones
> are united inseparably in Tara, mother of the victorious ones.
> The instant the piercing ray of her compassion strikes my
> heart
> it dispels all the darkness in my mind.
> After the pure realms, owing to my previous aspirations,
> had actually appeared clearly in the mirror of my heart,
> this fine and correct account, free of all exaggeration or
> deprecation
> and unharmed by the demons of sectarianism or jealousy,
> appeared solely by the grace of my lamas.
> Therefore, if we devotedly honor those sacred ones,
> the spiritual friends who show us the correct path,
> in all our lifetimes may they grant us their blessings.
>
> *Sarva mangalam*—may everything be auspicious.
> Good fortune, good fortune, good fortune!
> May auspiciousness blaze, and the world be adorned.
> *Jayantu*—may there be victory.

THE STAIRCASE TO LIBERATION

5

SUMMARY OF THE EFFECTS OF VIRTUE AND HARM

Hri Uncontrived and free of elaboration is the dharmakaya
   lama;
the supremely blissful enjoyment of the richness of being—
   sambhogakaya—is the lama, lord of dharma;
born on a long-stemmed lotus is the nirmanakaya lama:[1]
I pay homage to the vajra holder of the three kayas.

Flawless deity, your form white,
your head adorned with a perfectly awakened buddha,
gazing upon ordinary beings with eyes of innate compassion:
I pay homage to Avalokiteshvara.[2]
Refuge who gives birth to all victorious ones and the field in
   which they reveal their display,[3]
mother, venerable Tara, at your lotus feet,
until I attain enlightenment
I will take refuge with devotion, trusting completely in you.

ༀ Having been born to my kind mother, I, Dawa
Drolma, daughter of the Tromge family, treated all miserable
beings lovingly out of my compassion. During my fifteenth
year, I was afflicted by an illness; the mother, White Tara,
inspired me and completely assuaged my pains with a medicine that saved me from death. For a period of ten days and

nights,[4] I gave up eating and experienced prophetic visions that impelled me to seek what is virtuous. After the appearances of this lifetime and my awareness of them were arrested, four dakinis became my companions and bore me on a silken litter. For a short time we journeyed through the narrow passage of the bardo. I had terrifying visions, fleeting and indefinite; I saw, as well, several holy masters guiding beings from that state, and I conversed with them in a mood of both faith in their compassion and disillusionment with cyclic existence.

Om mani padme hung.

ཨོཾ།   The realm of the Mountain of Glory is shaped like a heart. In the midst of a city of dakinis on its imposing slopes, in the center of a many-storied, transparent immeasurable mansion, I met the glorious Orgyan and his retinue of emanations, the king of Tibet and his subjects.[5] With faith and yearning, I prostrated and entreated him to grant me refuge. He bestowed specific empowerments and blessings on me, his mind filled with compassionate affection. He said, "Do not forget the ways in which visions of the six classes of beings manifest for you; return to the human realm to entreat people to pursue virtue." Hosts of dakas and yoginis and the mother Tsogyal, dakini of pristine awareness, honored me by escorting me for one hundred paces. I touched their hearts with my noble prayers of aspiration.

With Tara, my guardian protector, to inspire me, I passed through the long and narrow defile of the bardo. There, I beheld fleeting and vague impressions of all manner of deceased beings (both those I knew and those I did not) swirling about together. Crying out sorrowfully, these wretched ones gave me many discouraging messages to take back to the world of the living they had left behind. They pleaded,

"Out of your fondness and compassion for us, please convey our messages." Grasping my hands, they shed torrents of tears. Unable to bear this, I repeated the mani mantra over and over.

Om mani padme hung.

ॐ As I journeyed through the afterworld of the dead, I saw how painful it was for those without the solace of the Buddhadharma. A bloody rain of weapons fell from the sky above and the surrounding space shuddered with a thunderous sound like a thousand dragons roaring, while on the ground fearsome denizens brandished cruel weapons and shouted, "Kill, kill! Beat, beat!" A great darkness of misery enveloped that region.

Om mani padme hung.

ॐ Those who had practiced the Buddhadharma were happy and content in the bardo. For them, the sky was filled with hundreds of rainbows and a sweet rain of nectar fell, while in all directions dakas and dakinis sang, danced, and played musical instruments, presenting clouds of offerings and leading these beings on the path to the supreme bliss of liberation. For them, a day of happiness dawned.

Om mani padme hung.

ॐ You in the world of the living, although you have gathered clothing for a hundred years, you will go forth naked on the morning of your death; better, then, to wear shabby clothes while practicing what is virtuous. Although you have amassed food for a long time, you will go hungry on the morning of your death; better, then, to make a gift even of your leftovers. Although you have amassed possessions throughout your life, you will go forth empty-handed on the morning of your death; better, then, to make provisions for your journey in future lifetimes. On that morning when the dark noose of the lord of death closes about you, and it is time for you to go, helplessly, your father and mother won't be there to protect you, your loving relatives and friends won't be there to shelter you. You will see that they are mere objects of your memories of happiness and joy, that they have no true essence. Cast off these bonds of appearances and perceptions based on confusion, for it is surely time to practice the divine Buddhadharma, which will truly benefit you in the future. Do not let the remainder of your human life slip away.

Om mani padme hung.

꧇ In yet another impure vision, I beheld vague, terrifying scenes of hell. Within a fearsome fortress of skulls, on a throne of skulls piled high, was the king of death, terrible and cruel. Many of his frightful minions were herding together countless beings who had died and were in the bardo. Each of these beings was accompanied by a fair child and a dark one, who were skilled at assessing virtuous and harmful deeds. Awa Langgo, the ox-headed minion, was skilled in reading the scroll records; the lion-headed minion, at beating the drum of karmic justice; the serpent-headed minion, at divining in a mirror; the stag-headed minion, at laying out the rack; the minion with the head of a red snow bear, at polishing the weapons; the monkey-headed minion, at measuring with the balance; the bear-headed minion, at distinguishing virtuous actions from harmful ones. These seven minions examined the deceased closely as to their positive and negative karma; singing praises of those who were spiritual, they led them along the luminous path to liberation.

Om mani padme hung.

〰️৹ৗ   Those without spiritual qualities were dragged downward by their hair along a path into darkness, while the minions cried out, "Kill them! Cut them! Beat them!" Destined for the hot and cold hells, they would be subjected to unremitting pain for an aeon.

Om mani padme hung.

〰️৹ৗ   My affection for beings made this impossible to bear; I chanted the mani and tare mantras to a plaintive melody, which brought some slight benefit to those connected to me by faith and yearning.

Om mani padme hung.

〰️৹ৗ   Dharmaraja stared intently at me and demanded, "Girl, what virtuous or harmful deeds have you committed? There is no benefit in concealing anything, so tell me!" My protector, Tara, rose and bowed respectfully, saying, "Ah! This girl has faith and respect, so do not be angry with her. She has treated those under her with compassion and loving kindness, and has always avoided harmful actions." Despite her request he said to me, "Reveal your virtuous and harmful actions."

The ox-headed minion scrutinized the scroll. "He, he! Although engaged in much activity, you have maintained your focus."

This girl said respectfully, "I have committed the fault of pushing unruly children onto the ground." As I said this, I felt a little fearful.

Dharmaraja, however, smiled slightly and said, "Although you might need to purify yourself of flaws, your attitude of love and protectiveness toward young children outshines any harmful action you may have committed. I can send you back to your realm. Now take your account of the hell realms, the messages sent by the dead, and my own commands to the world of the living and relate them clearly. It is timely for you, too, to confess your harmful actions and pursue what is virtuous. Henceforth make sure you do nothing to be ashamed of."

Om mani padme hung.

ༀ Although the dead sent back many messages, let me ask you gathered here to listen to the main points. You who have been left behind in this world of the living, positive and negative karma must inevitably be accounted for. Those wretched beings in lower realms of misery suffer continually with no chance of escape, so do not let your affection and compassion for them subside. Now is the time to dedicate some virtue swiftly on their behalf.

Om mani padme hung.

ༀ With regard to virtue, in intent and in actuality it is time to rely on the key points of gathering, purifying, and increasing.[6] To purify your obscurations, like getting up again by relying on the ground on which you have fallen, clearly visualize, honor, and worship the objects of your faith and offer confession. The three acts of writing out, reading, and spreading the commands of Dharmaraja, and especially the *Liberation Sutra*, the *Sutra of Threefold Purification*, the *Enumeration of Names of Buddhas*, the *Sutra of the Medicine Buddha*, the *Confession of Failings*, and the *Confession Tantra*, are the most noble ways to purify obscurations. Vajrasattva, the all-knowing Vairocana, the immutable Akshobhya, the rituals of the peaceful and wrathful deities, the ritual *Dredging the Pit of Hell from Its Depths*, Akashagarbha,[7] the *Sutra of Liberation*, and the two texts entitled "Stainless"—use these nine means of purifying obscurations in the sutra and tantra

approaches. Constantly, with faith and compassion, maintain
the three points of ongoing awareness[8] and recite the mani,
siddhi, and tare mantras, as well as the hundred-syllable
mantra. Fly prayer flags, carve mantras in stones, turn prayer
wheels, and perform the nyungnay fasting ritual. Rescue beings from harm, ransom the lives of beings destined to be
killed, and close off areas to hunters. Now is the time to
make offerings to support practitioners and tsog feasts. Make
an effort to ensure circumstances supportive of the practice
of dharma and to render service. If their relationships are not
weak, then the dead who are connected to the living through
family, dharma, or material objects will reap the benefit of
whatever virtue is dedicated to them. Persevere in dedicating
virtue in the names of specific individuals. If you act in this
way, the benefits will be great; in general, the living and the
dead share a fundamental common lot. I say to you, "Do not
forget the messages of the dead. Do not distance yourself
from them or neglect them." You who have understanding,
keep this in mind.

Om mani padme hung.

〜〜| Furthermore, the king of destiny made the following
commands:

All of you in the world of the living, high or low:
All that is born dies, and all that comes together falls apart.
The final outcome of gathering is dispersal, and the final
  outcome of rising is falling.
Since nothing in cyclic existence is permanent or stable,
do not cling to the seeming permanence of things or fixate
  on them as true.
Whatever appears to you is like the experiences in a dream;
do not be attached to illusory appearances of happiness.
If you want happiness, abandon distraction and laziness.

Develop renunciation, bodhicitta, and a pure outlook.
Devote the three avenues of your being[9] to what is wholly
    positive.
If you do not wish to suffer, purify the effects of former
    harmful deeds,
and firmly resolve not to commit them again.
The karmic results of positive and negative actions are
    infallible;
do not deny them with empty words.
You will be reborn in a land of darkness that lasts a great
    aeon.
Those with great desire and avarice will suffer from hunger
    and thirst in the preta realms for one million eight
    hundred thousand years.
Those with evil motivation and an obsession with killing
will experience the hot and cold hells for many aeons.
Those who commit negative actions against significant
    individuals,
who have committed acts of immediate karmic retribution,[10]
or who have abandoned the dharma or hold wrong views
    about it
will be reborn in Vajra Hell and remain there for an aeon,
    experiencing enormous suffering without interruption.
Those who are envious and competitive, or who delight in
    quarreling and strife,
will suffer for a long time in the realms of demigods.
Those whose minds are swollen with arrogance and whose
    good karma is subject to exhaustion
will be reborn among gods and will eventually fall from that
    state.
Those who engage in a mixture of avaricious and virtuous
    actions
will be reborn among humans subject to anxiety and want.
Om mani padme hung.

Therefore, without falling into harmful actions, the eight
    worldly preoccupations,[11]

or inconsequential states of mind,
make an effort to plant roots of virtue that are totally pure.
Om mani padme hung.

Hidden karma caused by actions done in secret becomes
    obvious when it falls on top of you.
The choice between good and evil is in your hands.
If you do not think about this, regret will be useless when
    you arrive before me, the lord of death, in my court of
    justice.
Om mani padme hung.

As you have seen, I gather many spirits of the dead as
    minions.
We pierce beings with our sharp weapons,
we make them drink cauldrons of molten metal,
we cause them to suffer agonies of heat and cold for aeons,
we ensure that the suffering goes on without interruption.
Om mani padme hung.

Do not forget these messages; convey them clearly.
This will bring you great merit.
You monastics and laypeople gathered here,
I ask that you reflect on these matters over and over again
    until you are certain of their meaning.
Om mani padme hung.

༄༅། I ask the sources of refuge, victorious ones and their
heirs, to be my witnesses. May all the virtue that I and others
gather throughout the three times, as exemplified by the virtuous potential of faith and devotion gathered here, be dedicated together, and by the force of this dedication may the
teachings of victorious ones, the theoretical and the experi-
ential, flourish to the furthest limits in all directions. May the
enlightened intentions of lamas, our glorious lord protectors, be fulfilled. May all victorious ones and their heirs be glad-
dened by offerings. May the enlightened activities of holy

people who hold the teachings flourish. May the sacred bonds with those who guard the teachings be fulfilled through sacred substances. May the view and conduct of the sangha that maintains the teachings be pure. May the power and influence of those who respect the teachings increase. May the degeneration of the animate and inanimate world be pacified. I dedicate this virtue in order to bring about healing now and in the future.

I dedicate this virtue to my two parents, as well as to enemies, demons, hindrances, and all those connected to me through positive or negative karma, and especially to those men and women who depend on me for their livelihood, the horses that serve us by plowing our fields, the cows that supply us with the distillation of their essence, and those whose flesh and blood and hide we use—all sentient beings whose deaths we have caused directly or indirectly. I dedicate this virtue so that all the harmful actions and failings that we and others have committed, or caused to be committed, or rejoiced at, along with the habitual patterns that underlie them, may be purified swiftly. I dedicate this virtue so that all beings in the six classes and the bardo may easily and swiftly perfect the two great accumulations, and so realize directly the all-pervasive and fundamental nature of reality, attaining unsurpassable enlightenment that makes evident the qualities of renunciation and maturation.

ༀ This summary of the visions of hell realms was composed in the manner of turning the wheel[12] by an actual emanation of Tsogyal, the dakini Sherab Chhödron, also known as Dawa Drolma.

Sarva mangalam—Good fortune, good fortune, good fortune! May everything be auspicious.

NOTES

1. Copper-Colored Mountain of Glory

1 The first folio of the manuscript is missing, and so the translation begins on folio 2a. This passage seems to be part of the introductory verses, specifically Dawa Drolma's statement of intent.

2 A well-known prayer to Padmasambhava. Also known as Guru Rinpoche, Padmasambhava was a Vajrayana Buddhist master of the Indian subcontinent who journeyed to Tibet in the eighth century C.E. to further establish the Buddhist tradition in that land. He is revered by Tibetans as the "second Buddha," and much of the devotional practice in Tibetan Buddhism focuses on him.

3 *Dakini* is a Sanskrit term used in Vajrayana Buddhism to denote either a feminine deity embodying enlightened activity or, on a more mundane level, a human woman who has attained a remarkable level of spiritual accomplishment. The masculine equivalent is *daka.*

Dorje Yudron is one of the twelve *tanma* goddesses who have sworn to protect the Buddhist religion and the Tibetan nation.

4 Mahayana Buddhism recognizes ten levels of realization between the first glimpse of the emptiness that is the true nature of reality and the fully awakened level of a buddha. A bodhisattva is, in a general sense, one who is following the Mahayana path and, more technically, a being who has attained at least the first level of realization.

5 Local gods are powerful nonhuman beings who inhabit and

hold dominion over specific regions, controlling weather and soil conditions. In Tibetan culture much attention was paid to maintaining harmonious relations with the local gods of one's area. Nyens are powerful martial earth spirits.

6 In Tibetan Buddhism, tulkus are incarnations of former spiritual masters, formally recognized and enthroned and educated to carry on the activities of their former incarnations. The three tulkus mentioned here were Tromge Kundun, Tromge Trungpa, and Drimed Khakyod Wangpo, who were teachers of Dawa Drolma and figure prominently in her accounts. The last was, moreover, her paternal uncle and had passed away before the events narrated herein took place.

7 Jatrul, the "incarnation of Ja," a student of the three tulkus mentioned in note 6, claimed that Dawa Drolma was destined to be his spiritual consort. Her family, however, refused to give him her hand in marriage. Bitterly disappointed, Jatrul blamed Dawa Drolma's father, Jigmed T'hrogyal, for denying him his destined wife.

8 When human beings break their Vajrayana commitments, or *samaya*, they are reborn as nonhuman demonic beings known in Tibetan as *damsri*, or "demons of broken samaya." Not only do these demons experience the negative effects of their own breaches of ethics, they encourage others by their actions to commit the same breaches.

9 The three planes are the nether world, the surface world, and the heavens.

10 A karmic deity is the deity with whom a person has the strongest karmic connection, owing to ties established in former lifetimes.

11 Orgyan is the Tibetan name for the Sanskrit Oddiyana, which refers to a legendary country the inhabitants of which are advanced practitioners of Vajrayana Buddhism. The most reliable accounts identify it with the area of present-day Kashmir.

12 Tormas are certain offering rituals performed in the Tibetan Buddhist tradition.

13 Dawa Drolma is speaking of Tromge Kundun, whom she also refers to later as Chhogtrul Rinpoche, the "Precious Sublime

Emanation." One's root lama is the teacher who points out the true nature of one's own mind.

14 Tromge Monastery, in which Dawa Drolma's teachers lived and taught, followed both the Nyingma and Sakya lineages of Tibetan Buddhism.

15 A major tantra (see note 61) and deity of the highest class of tantras in the "new" schools of Tibetan Buddhism founded since the eleventh century. Hevajra is a central practice in the Sakya lineage.

16 Vajradhara is a buddha of *dharmakaya*, or ultimate reality, in Vajrayana symbolism.

17 Throughout her narratives Dawa Drolma refers to herself in the third person as "this girl." This seems to be due as much to the fact that she dictated these accounts to a scribe as to her modesty and self-effacement.

18 Amitayus is the buddha of longevity, whose practice extends one's life span. Samyak and Vajrakilaya are wrathful deities whose meditations protect one against obstacles.

There are pure realms associated with the three *kaya*s, or levels of enlightened being. The Copper-Colored Mountain of Glory is one of many so-called *nirmanakaya* pure realms, existing in some sense in a manner analogous to our own ordinary level of physical reality, but accessible only to people with deep spiritual insight and attainment. *Sambhogakaya* pure realms constitute an ongoing level of pure noncorporeal form. The pure realm of *dharmakaya* is the formless, fundamental nature of reality, beyond any conceptual elaboration. Dawa Drolma's experiences in this chapter take place entirely within the context of a nirmanakaya pure realm, although her guide, Tara, refers to the other two levels later in this chapter (see p. 19 and note 83).

19 An empowerment is a ritual in Vajrayana Buddhism that authorizes the recipient to practice a specific deity meditation.

A terton is one who rediscovers and reveals hidden treasure teachings, or *termas*. Laykyi Dorje was a Nyingma teacher of the fourteenth century who discovered a number of important cycles of such teachings.

20 In genuine experiences of intrinsic awareness, one may suddenly know events, languages, concepts, and so forth that one had been previously ignorant of.

21 That is, 1924.

22 These are the teachings of Vajrayana Buddhism, "secret" because they are both profound (and therefore accessible only with proper guidance) and intended to be kept private between teacher and student. The use of "mantra" figures prominently in such teachings, but the etymology of the term indicates "that which guards the mind" against confused thought patterns.

23 Focusing on a form of Avalokiteshvara, the bodhisattva of compassion, with eleven faces, one thousand arms, and one thousand eyes, this is usually a two-day ritual, with a partial fast on the first day and a total fast on the second.

24 These are the two stages of formal Vajrayana meditation. The former is concerned primarily with visualization and mantra repetition; the latter deals more with advanced yogic techniques and formless meditation.

25 Bhurkakuta is a deity associated with the purification of broken or impure samaya.

26 For an explanation of the six realms, see the Introduction.

27 This major cycle was a terma discovered by the terton Karma Lingpa in the fourteenth century.

28 The mantra of Avalokiteshvara, the bodhisattva of compassion: *Om mani padme hung.* It is also referred to as the "six-syllable mantra."

29 Different times of day are associated with the four kinds of enlightened activity—early morning with pacification, late morning with enrichment, afternoon and early evening with power, and later evening with wrathful energy.

30 These are liturgies focusing on Yeshe Tsogyal, the Tibetan consort of Padmasambhava. The offering of a feast is a central ritual in Vajrayana Buddhism, practiced to enhance one's realization and to atone for infractions of one's spiritual commitments.

31 This statement is a reference to an axiomatic view of Bud-

dhism: Given that all beings' mindstreams have undergone a beginningless series of incarnations in lifetime after lifetime, it follows that all beings have at one time been one's own father or mother.

32 The "great Orgyan" refers to Padmasambhava, because his miraculous birth occurred in the land of Orgyan. The Three Jewels are the highest spiritual principles of the Buddhist path—buddha, or enlightened mind (as embodied, for example, in the historical buddha Shakyamuni); dharma, the teachings given by such a buddha that lead others to enlightenment; and sangha, those who practice and realize these teachings and so can function as guides and companions on the spiritual path.

33 Bodhicitta (the "awakening" or "enlightening attitude") comprises two aspects—a relative one of altruistic compassion and an ultimate one of realization of emptiness as the true nature of phenomena.

34 This measure was taken to provide convincing evidence that her delog experience had been genuine, not an elaborate hoax.

35 A level of obscuration resulting from the trauma to the mind in the *bardo*, or intermediate state between death and rebirth, during conception, gestation, and birth. This accounts in part for the fact that tulkus may not exhibit total recall of previous lifetimes.

36 A Vajrayana deity particularly associated with purification of the effects of harmful actions and obscurations.

37 Drolma, the Tibetan equivalent of the Sanskrit Tara, is commonly given to women in Tibet. Tsult'hrim Drolma was a nun who cared for and taught Chagdud Rinpoche when he was a child (and, he wryly recalls, spanked him a great deal).

38 In Vajrayana Buddhism, the five "buddha families" are a means of classifying the deities used in meditation; they also constitute the schema for the transformation of impure factors in one's ordinary makeup into their pure and authentic aspects. Here the blue color of Dawa Drolma's head covering indicates the vajra family, symbolizing the transformation of

anger into its pure aspect of pristine awareness, which reflects everything clearly like a mirror.

39 Another honorific title for Tromge Kundun.

40 A group of five goddesses, originally worldly spirits but tamed by Padmasambhava to be protectors of the Buddhist teachings. Associated with the area around Mount Everest, they are worshiped throughout the Tibetan world.

41 Dispelling Obstacles on the Path is a well-known devotional prayer, part of a terma cycle discovered in the fourteenth century. The vajra guru is the mantra of Padmasambhava: *Om ah hung vajra guru padma siddhi hung.* The mantra of the white and green forms of Tara is *Om tara tuttare ture soha.* The mantra of the red form of Tara is *Om tare tam soha.*

42 All of these details were specified in Tara's prophecy to Dawa Drolma.

43 The karma created by slaying an animal taints such clothing and would have interfered with the success of her delog experience.

44 Rain falling in certain seasons associated with the constellation of the *rishis,* or seers, is gathered and stored by Tibetans for its medicinal properties.

45 The term *kunzhi* (the Tibetan equivalent of the Sanskrit *alaya*) here refers to a preconscious level devoid of even subtle conceptual thoughts.

46 These three kinds of experience arise in meditation as provisional signs of success, but one must not fixate upon them as goals in themselves, for this will limit one's spiritual progress. Fixating upon bliss brings about rebirth as a god in the desire realm; upon clarity, rebirth as a god in the form realm; upon nonconceptual awareness, rebirth as a god in the formless realm—all realms within conditioned existence.

47 As used here, "ordinariness" denotes that which is fundamental, genuine, and uncontrived.

48 In Vajrayana rituals, a beribboned arrow symbolizes longevity and prosperity.

49 In Buddhist cosmology, our world system consists of a central mountain surrounded by four major continents, each of which

is flanked on either side by minor continents, or subcontinents. The subcontinent to the southwest of the central mountain and west of our world (the "southern continent") is Chamara. Padmasambhava resides there, subduing a race of bloodthirsty demons that would otherwise overrun our world.

50 The cloud imagery expresses the vast and ethereal quality of her experience.

51 The residence of Padmasambhava in his pure realm.

52 The Sanskrit term *vidyadhara* (holder of intrinsic awareness) refers to one who has discovered the true nature of his or her own mind as an intrinsic state of enlightened awareness (and thus "holds" this experience).

53 "Lake-Born Vajra of Orgyan," a common epithet of Padmasambhava.

54 Vajravarahi is a feminine deity of the highest class of tantras in Vajrayana Buddhism.

55 The Sanskrit term *tathagata* (one who has arrived at a state of suchness) is an epithet for a buddha.

56 It has not been possible to identify this figure; he seems to have been an actual historical personage of Dawa Drolma's acquaintance.

57 A mala is a string of beads used like a rosary to count mantras or prayers.

58 Reciting the hundred-syllable mantra of the deity Vajrasattva is a Vajrayana technique for purifying oneself of the effects of harmful actions and obscurations.

59 This is the longest version of a description of the universe from an ideal, stylized point of view; this universe, summoned up in one's imagination, is offered to the object of one's faith as a means of gaining merit and deepening insight.

60 The woman being bathed was a dakini by virtue of having been reborn in the pure realm of Padmasambhava due to her spiritual attainment.

61 The sutras are the discourses of the Buddha that form the scriptural basis of the exoteric schools of Hinayana and Mahayana Buddhism; the tantras are the more secret scriptures that form the basis of Vajrayana Buddhist teachings.

62 A great master who lived from 1820 to 1892. He was instrumental in leading an ecumenical reform movement, centered in eastern Tibet in the nineteenth century. Although he was nominally a lama of the Sakya school, he studied widely and transmitted lineages in all schools of Tibetan Buddhism.

63 These are the sutras, or discourses, of the Buddha; the vinaya, or ethical codes; and the abhidharma, or metaphysical and psychological teachings.

64 The vajra and bell are implements held in the hands during the performance of Vajrayana rituals. The vajra symbolizes skillful means, the bell transcendent knowledge of emptiness.

65 A reference to the common Tibetan custom of offering a scarf of white cloth to a teacher when requesting an audience or a formal transmission of spiritual teachings. Symbolic of one's pure sincerity, the scarf is often placed back around one's neck by the teacher as a blessing.

66 Derge served as the major cultural and administrative center of eastern Tibet. The dakini referred to here was an actual woman who lived before Dawa Drolma's time.

67 Part of a cycle of terma teachings, some of which have been translated into English as the *Tibetan Book of the Dead*.

68 A chapter of a tantra used in the Nyingma school of Tibetan Buddhism as a popular confession liturgy.

69 A form of breath retention widely used in advanced Vajrayana meditation practices.

70 These three practices are contained in a cycle of terma teachings called the *Heart Drop of Longchenpa* (*Longchen Nying-t'hig*), revealed in the seventeenth century by Rigdzin Jigmed Lingpa. For information on this cycle, see H. H. Dilgo Khyentse Rinpoche, *The Wish-Fulfilling Jewel* (Boston: Shambhala, 1988), p. 9; and Tulku Thondup, *The Tantric Tradition of the Nyingmapa* (Marion, Mass.: Buddhayana, 1984), p. 174.

71 That is, her paternal uncle, Drimed Khakyod Wangpo.

72 The daughter of the king of Zahor in India, Mandarava was a spiritual consort of Padmasambhava who aided him in gaining power over longevity.

73 This is a well-known modified version of the Seven-Line Supplication.

74 Maras are forces or beings that limit one's experience and bind one to cyclic existence. Four such maras are commonly cited: the afflictive emotions, death (personified as Yama, lord of death), the psychophysical aggregates that constitute the mind-body of a spiritually unawakened individual, and forces that inhibit the mind's ability to attain higher levels of meditative absorption (personified as "the children of the gods").

75 In Vajrayana Buddhism, white and blue are associated with the east, yellow with the south, red with the west, and green with the north.

76 Literally, "about [the length of] a sleeve."

77 The terma marks (≋) indicate that various quotations in this account constitute a kind of terma, or mind treasure, that Dawa Drolma is revealing.

78 In the Nyingma system of Tibetan Buddhism, Samantabhadra is the embodiment of dharmakaya—ultimate reality, indescribable and ineffable. The term connotes that which is "wholly positive."

79 Lotus King (Padma Gyalpo) and Padma T'hod T'hreng Tzal are epithets for specific aspects of Padmasambhava.

80 A yogini of ancient Buddhist India who figured prominently in the transmission of many Nyingmapa teachings. See Thondup, *The Tantric Tradition of the Nyingmapa*, p. 17.

81 A metaphor for the integration of skillful means and transcendent knowledge.

82 The Sanskrit terms *samsara* and *nirvana* denote, respectively, the unenlightened, conditioned state of ordinary existence versus the enlightened, unconditioned state of a buddha's awareness.

83 This statement indicates that Dawa Drolma has not actually died, but must return to her body in the human realm. Although Tara makes reference at this point to other pure realms of the sambhogakaya and dharmakaya levels of enlightened being, all the events in this chapter, including those

from this point on, take place within the nirmanakaya pure realm of the Copper-Colored Mountain of Glory.

84 These five kinds of certainty are the distinguishing characteristics of the sambhogakaya—that there is always a perfect teacher, retinue, environment, teaching, and occasion.

85 An epithet for Avalokiteshvara, the bodhisattva of compassion.

86 That is, the dharmakaya buddha, Samantabhadra.

87 One of the seventeen main tantras of the ati yoga, or Great Perfection, approach of the Nyingma school.

88 She obviously felt that the benefits of recounting her experiences outweighed the consequences of violating Tara's injunction.

89 According to Chagdud Rinpoche, this may refer to the mandala of the five aspects of Padma T'hod T'hreng Tzal.

90 The Samantabhadra referred to in this well-known metaphor of the ideal act of making offerings is not the dharmakaya buddha, but a bodhisattva renowned in the sutras for his ability to create offerings at will through his powers of meditative absorption.

91 The gods in this heaven of the desire realm in cyclic existence (the name literally means "Enjoying Emanations") have such enormous stores of merit that they can effortlessly emanate whatever sense pleasures they wish.

92 The trident is a symbol for the attainment of the three kayas.

93 This is a common metaphor for the inadequacy of ordinary language and concepts to express the direct experience of one's true nature.

94 One who maintains the three levels of commitment in Buddhist practice—the precepts of the Hinayana path for individual liberation, the bodhisattva vow of the Mahayana path, and the tantric samaya of the Vajrayana path.

95 Srongtzan Gampo was the ruler of the Tibetan region during much of the seventh century. Buddhism was introduced to Tibet during his reign, although the consolidation of a Tibetan tradition of Buddhism took place several centuries later. Nub Namnying (or Namkhai Nyingpo) was one of the twenty-five

most intimate students of Padmasambhava in Tibet. Dagpo Daod was more commonly known as Gampopa, the main student of Milarepa and a founder of the Kagyud school of Tibetan Buddhism, who lived from 1079 to 1153.

96 That is, when Dawa Drolma had known him in the human realm before his death.

97 A Tibetan teacher and terton who spent much of his life in Sikkim. He lived from 1597 to around 1650.

98 Dzaga Monastery was a large Nyingma monastery about a day's travel from Tromge Monastery in Dawa Drolma's home region of T'hromt'har. There was a strong connection between the two centers. A heart son or daughter is a very close student.

99 The four visions are stages of realization in the Great Perfection approach. The terms "original purity" and "spontaneous presence" refer here to the two stages of practice in the Great Perfection, called t'hregchhod and t'högal in Tibetan.

100 The same word in Tibetan can refer to human thighbones fashioned into trumpets and to similar instruments made of brass and copper.

101 That is, the Nyingma school. The ritual referred to is part of a major cycle of terma teachings revealed in the twelfth century by Nyang Nyima Odzer.

102 The metaphor is intended to express swift and unhesitating movement in a specific direction.

103 Gain and loss, fame and disgrace, praise and blame, and pleasure and pain.

104 These are Sanskrit vowels.

105 A ritual in which a high lama's death is rehearsed in a symbolic way, with offerings and an effigy being presented in his or her stead to satisfy the forces that could otherwise threaten the lama's life span. A main element in the ritual is the dance of the five dakinis, performed by five young women, who are turned back with offerings rather than allowed to conduct the consciousness of the lama to a pure realm.

106 That is, "When will you be reborn in the human realm?"

107 Teachings codified by Chetzun Sengge Wangkhyug (eleventh to twelfth centuries) upon his attainment of "rainbow body" at the age of 125. They were revealed by Jamyang Khyentsei Wangpo (1820–1892).

Rainbow body is the highest attainment from the perspective of the Great Perfection, or Dzogchen, approach, in which the practitioner's corporeal body transforms into a body of rainbow light, which is accessible as a guiding force only to people of very great spiritual accomplishment and remains until samsara is emptied of beings.

108 Since to do so would be to risk actual death, with the consequent inability of her consciousness to re-enter her body.

109 Pills that have been consecrated in special ceremonies and that transmit blessings to those who ingest them.

110 A repa is a yogin who wears only a thin, white cotton garment (such as Milarepa).

111 This is a well-known verse from the Tibetan translation of the *Bodhicharyavatara*, a famous work on Mahayana Buddhism by Shantideva of India.

112 Literally, "by mouth or hand."

113 According to Chagdud Rinpoche, this is probably a reference to fierce gatekeepers that Dawa Drolma might encounter on her journey back to the human world; the rice is a form of protection.

114 See note 111 above.

115 Lantza is a decorative script used by Tibetans on the title pages of books and for inscriptions on prayer wheels and so forth; it was a north Indian script upon which the so-called headed (*uchen*) letters of the Tibetan alphabet were based. Wardhu (Wartula Gupta) script was another north Indian script upon which the "headless" (*umed*) letters of Tibetan are based.

116 A district in the southern Tibetan province of Dagpo.

117 This is the individual also referred to as Jatrul; see note 7 above.

2. Reflections in the Crystal Mirror

1 Fear of lions, wild elephants, fire, snakes, floods, imprisonment, thieves, and cannibals.

2 That is, Tromge Kundun, Tromge Trungpa, and Drimed Khakyod Wangpo, the three tulkus who are first mentioned in Chapter 1 and who figure prominently in Dawa Drolma's accounts.

3 The Tibetan term *bardo* means "an interval between two points"; throughout this text it refers specifically to the interval between death and rebirth, during which time the karmic forces in an individual's makeup create projections that foreshadow that being's future rebirth.

4 Because of one's attachments to them, one becomes ensnared in activities and concerns that perpetuate cyclic existence.

5 The concept of refuge is fundamental to Buddhism; indeed, the "vow of refuge" is the first formal step in an individual's personal commitment to the Buddhist path. One takes refuge in the "Three Jewels," three spiritual ideals or principles (see Chapter 1, note 32). Thus, granting refuge implies more than simply sheltering or protecting someone, because spiritual inspiration and guidance are involved.

6 The white and green forms of Tara.

7 An epithet for Manjushri, the bodhisattva of wisdom.

8 Sodnam Tzemo, who lived from 1142 to 1182, was the son of Sachhen Kunga Nyingpo (founder of the Sakya school of Tibetan Buddhism), and thus was the second of the five "founding fathers" of the school.

9 The second syllable of the name Gyajam is a contraction of Jamyang, the Tibetan form of the Sanskrit name Manjughosha.

10 A metaphor for a scene of chaos and upset.

11 The two texts mentioned are used in purification rituals in the Tibetan Buddhist tradition.

12 The "king of destiny," an epithet of Yama.

13 The "board of fate" is depicted as a flat, paddle-like club marked with lines etched in a crosshatch pattern; each

individual's destiny is connected with a mark inscribed in one of the resulting squares. The mirror of karma clearly reflects one's deeds in the preceding lifetime, allowing no tampering with the inexorable law of karma.

14 A superstition existed in certain parts of Tibet that a person who poisoned a lama to death in some way took on the spiritual merit of the deceased. But the actual result of the deed was rebirth in hell.

15 The first of the eight hot hells of traditional Buddhist cosmology. For descriptions of the hells and preta realms referred to in this chapter, see *The Jewel Ornament of Liberation*, H. V. Guenther, trans. (Boston: Shambhala, 1986), pp. 55–69; *Künzang La-may Zhal-lung*, S. T. Kazi, trans. (Upper Montclair, N.J.: Diamond-Lotus Publishing, 1989), pp. 83–139; and Patrul Rinpoche, *The Words of My Perfect Teacher* (San Francisco: HarperCollins, 1994), pp. 63–76.

16 Pretas are tormented spirits afflicted by extreme hunger and thirst and exposure to the elements.

17 A buddha whose meditation and mantra are particularly efficacious in purifying the effects of harmful actions.

18 See Chapter 1, note 62.

19 According to traditional Buddhist cosmology, Mount Sumeru is the central mountain of our world system.

20 Three kinds of virtuous actions are physical—preserving life, generosity, and sexual morality; four are verbal—being truthful, speaking kindly, promoting harmony with one's speech, and speaking meaningful words; and three are mental—contentment, benevolence, and correct understanding of spiritual truths.

21 Tibetans believe that prayer flags send the blessings of the prayers on the wind, benefiting all whom the wind touches.

22 The siddhi mantra is another name for the Padmasambhava mantra, *Om ah hung vajra guru padma siddhi hung.*

23 A popular act of virtue in Tibet was to carve the six syllables of the mantra *Om mani padme hung* on stones, which were often piled up in cairns or walls.

24 Satsas are small clay replicas of *stupas*—monuments whose ar-

chitectural features represent aspects of enlightened mind—or deities cast in clay; the clay is often mixed with ashes from the remains of deceased individuals to transmit blessings to the deceased.

25 That is, images, books, and implements as symbolic receptacles of the form, speech, and mind of enlightened being.

26 In traditional Buddhist cosmology, one thousand world systems similar to our own collectively constitute a universe of the first order of magnitude; one thousand of these universes constitute a universe of the second order; and one thousand of these universes (that is, one billion world systems similar to our own) constitute a universe of the third order, a "three-thousand-fold universe."

27 The three realms are the desire realm (comprising the realms of hell beings, pretas, animals, humans, demigods, and the lower levels of gods), the subtler form realm (the middle levels of gods), and the most subtle formless realm (the highest levels of gods). All three realms are within the cycles of conditioned existence, thus representing no final happiness or liberation, and are still under the sway of the lord of death.

28 The three planes are another way of describing the cycle of existence; they are the netherworld, the surface world, and the heavens.

29 The "southern continent" of the four continents surrounding Mount Sumeru is our own human world, that is, roughly equivalent to the "Earth."

30 In dying, these highly realized individuals had offset the karma of many people that would ordinarily have resulted in their deaths.

31 A kind of tree growing in one of the so-called neighboring hells and constituting the primary source of suffering for beings in that realm. See Kazi, *Kün-zang La-may Zhal-lung*, pp. 93–94.

32 Literally, "the translated word [of the Buddha]." The Tibetan Buddhist canon, usually in 108 volumes, of the scriptures accepted as the teachings of the Buddha Shakyamuni.

33 Presumably her daughter is prone to anger and taking life.

34 These "children" are projections of the positive and negative elements in one's own makeup.

35 A reference to severe forms of corporal punishment that he, as the chieftain, was responsible for ordering.

36 A major figure in the Nyingma school of Tibetan Buddhism in the late nineteenth and early twentieth centuries.

37 That is, ordained clergy; yellow was a color reserved for the garments of monks and nuns in Tibet.

38 That is, without taking others with her on the merits of her positive karma.

39 A major monastic and political center in the southern Tibetan province of Tsang and the eponymous seat of the Sakya school of Tibetan Buddhism.

40 The accumulations of merit on the conventional level and pristine awareness on the ultimate level.

41 Manjushri, Avalokiteshvara, and Vajrapani (the bodhisattvas of wisdom, compassion, and spiritual power, respectively) are the bodhisattvas of the "three families"—that is, of the form, speech, and mind of all buddhas.

42 Benefit for oneself and others in the short and long term.

43 Even a negative involvement, due to a harmful action or ill-will toward someone, establishes a beneficial connection.

44 These are the opposites of the virtuous actions mentioned in note 20 above: the physical acts of killing, stealing, and sexual misconduct; the verbal acts of lying, speaking abusively, calumny, and idle gossip; and the mental acts of covetousness, ill-will, and wrong views concerning spiritual truths.

45 A large town (called Ta-chien-lu in Chinese) on the Tibetan–Chinese border, formerly the main point through which Chinese tea was imported into Tibetan territory.

46 Pretas with inner obscurations are those whose subjective perceptions are so distorted that although they are able to find food or drink, these turn to fire, filth, or poison when ingested.

47 A tantrika is a practitioner of the path of tantra, that is, Vajrayana Buddhism.

48 This refers to those who have received the same empower-

ments into Vajrayana practice from the same lamas; it is held
that no stronger bond can exist between people.

49 Vajra Hell is the realm into which beings fall due to grave infractions of their samaya commitments.

50 Buddhas who have appeared in the past, those who are appearing in the present, and those who will appear in the future.

51 Of body, speech, and mind.

52 Here the ordinary duality of positive and negative is replaced
by the higher principles of spiritual practice.

53 As the following lines make clear, this saint was Yeshe Dorje's
principal spiritual teacher.

54 The eight hot hells, eight cold hells, neighboring hells, and
temporary hells.

55 The Sanskrit equivalent of the name Yeshe Dorje.

56 Because Shakyamuni Buddha was sitting under a pipal (or
bodhi) tree when he attained enlightenment, the seeds are
prized as beads for malas.

57 It was common in Tibet to sponsor someone to read scriptures
aloud and dedicate the merit of the reading to the welfare of
the sponsor.

58 A large meadow near Dawa Drolma's home.

59 That is, the Buddha.

60 In Tibetan Buddhist practice, the name of one's lama is often
used in the sentence "___ knows all!" as a form of mantra.
Here the man is equating his teacher with Dorje Chang (Sanskrit Vajradhara), the dharmakaya buddha of ultimate truth.

61 The five emotional poisons are desire-attachment, anger, ignorance, pride, and envy.

62 P'howa, or the "transfer of consciousness," is a Vajrayana
technique that may be performed for oneself or for another's
benefit. It enables the consciousness to leave the body at
death in the most skillful and effective way to aid one's spiritual progress.

63 See Chapter 1, note 22.

64 By honoring them, others gather the accumulations of merit
and pristine awareness.

65 That is, consorts of lamas.

66 The four degrees of joy that arise successively in meditation are termed joy, sublime joy, special joy, and coemergent joy (or joy beyond [ordinary conditioned] joy).

67 Five acts whose karmic consequences are so severe that, without purification, they entail rebirth in a hell realm immediately upon the death of the one who has committed the act, without the usual bardo state intervening between death and rebirth. They are patricide, matricide, murder of an arhat (see Chapter 3, note 32), maliciously causing a buddha to bleed, and causing irreparable schisms in the Buddhist community.

68 That is, moral conduct that accepts certain forms of behavior as virtuous and rejects others as nonvirtuous.

69 Mamos are fierce goddesses.

3. Potala Mountain

1 See Chapter 1, note 55.

2 The eight qualities are coolness, sweetness, lightness, softness, clarity, freedom from impurities, digestibility, and soothing properties for the throat. The water of pure realms is traditionally described as having these qualities.

3 The five-layered walls are symbolic of the five buddha families central to the Vajrayana. Similarly, every "architectural" feature of these mansions symbolizes a particular factor or quality of spiritual practice and realization.

4 The wheel of dharma is an auspicious emblem fashioned of gold with eight spokes representing the noble eightfold path of Buddhism: correct view, realization, speech, conduct, livelihood, effort, mindfulness, and meditative absorption.

5 The makara is a mythological aquatic creature somewhat resembling a crocodile, used as a motif in Buddhist architecture.

6 See Chapter 1, note 91.

7 The form of a buddha is traditionally described as being adorned with thirty-two major and eighty minor marks of physical perfection that are the outward expressions of various inner spiritual qualities.

8 This spotted black antelope is traditionally held to be exceptionally gentle and compassionate.

9 That is, with the top side of the right foot placed on the left thigh and the top side of the left foot placed on the right thigh.

10 The traditional idiom "to turn the wheel of the dharma" denotes the activity of giving Buddhist teachings.

11 This refers to the traditional method of dividing a twenty-four-hour period into six "watches" of four hours each.

12 The Buddha prophesied that his teachings would endure in this world over ten periods of five hundred years each after his passing into nirvana. Each successive period would involve a more superficial and vague approach to the study and practice of these teachings, until only traces were left, following which they would disappear from this world until the next Buddha, Maitreya, appeared to introduce them once again.

13 Most philosophical views tend toward either the extreme of eternalism (naively affirming the existence of things just as they appear) or nihilism (just as naively denying that things exist at all). The "Middle Way" of the Buddha avoids these extremes by affirming interdependence as the process that accounts for the arising of phenomena in the conventional sense, while at the same time affirming that these phenomena lack any true self-nature.

14 That is, a body in a fortunate state of rebirth.

15 The six perfections (also known in Sanskrit as *paramitas*) are qualities that constitute the essence of the Mahayana path of Buddhism: generosity, discipline, patience, diligence, meditative stability, and transcendent knowledge.

16 The four methods of influencing others positively are giving generously of what is necessary, speaking in a pleasant manner, engaging in activities that benefit others, and acting in accord with the customs and expectations of others.

17 Knowledge arising from hearing teachings, contemplating, and meditating.

18 Mindfulness, alertness, heedfulness, and spiritual practice.

19 These are temporary vows, usually taken for twenty-four

hours, often in conjunction with the nyungnay fasting ritual. The eight vows are to avoid taking life, stealing, lying, engaging in sexual activity, eating at inappropriate times (before sunrise and after midday), wearing cosmetics or adornments, using high seats or thrones, and singing, dancing, or playing music.

20 Your body, speech, and mind.

21 See Chapter 1, note 103.

22 Physical, verbal, and mental.

23 This verse, a quotation from a sutra, is a well-known prayer of aspiration in all traditions of Tibetan Buddhism.

24 A well-known prayer of aspiration.

25 The pure realm associated with the western direction, known in Tibetan as Dewachan, or Realm of Bliss.

26 The *Saddharma-pundarika Sutra*, or *Lotus Sutra*, which exists in several English translations.

27 *Arya-karandavyuha Sutra.* A sutra dealing with the bodhisattva Avalokiteshvara and explaining the benefits of practice associated with this bodhisattva and the mantra *Om mani padme hung.*

28 Denizens who torment pretas and increase their suffering.

29 Shravakas and pratyekabuddhas are those who practice and realize the Hinayana path of Buddhist practice, as distinct from bodhisattvas, who attain buddhahood through the Mahayana path. Gods, celestial musicians, and so forth are various kinds of unenlightened beings within the cycle of conditioned existence; Ishvara and Maheshvara are powerful gods. Vajrapani is the bodhisattva of spiritual power.

30 A dharani is a kind of mantra, typically a long proselike formula that deals with the qualities of a particular deity or aspect of enlightenment.

31 See Chapter 2, note 67.

32 An arhat (literally, "one who has conquered the [inner] foe") has gained a partial degree of enlightenment by following the Hinayana approach of Buddhist practice. He or she has realized the nonexistence of the self of the individual personality, and so has transcended suffering and the causes of future suf-

fering. The drawback is that this level of realization provides only personal release from cyclic existence, and not the compassion and skillful means to liberate others.

4. Yulokod

1 See Chapter 2, note 40.
2 A reference to her journey to the pure realm of Avalokiteshvara.
3 "I pay homage to the exalted Tara."
4 See Chapter 3, note 2.
5 Gold, silver, coral, pearl, and turquoise or sapphire.
6 Through being seen, heard, touched, or remembered.
7 The heartwood of the sandalwood tree.
8 A secret name is bestowed by a guru upon a practitioner during an empowerment into one of the formal meditation techniques of Vajrayana Buddhism.
9 In Vajrayana terminology, the arising of joy in meditation is described as occurring in sixteen distinct stages. The image of a youth or young woman of sixteen years of age is employed to epitomize this process.
10 The immeasurable attitudes are love, compassion, joy, and equanimity.
11 A reference to the legend that the white and green forms of Tara sprang from tears shed by Avalokiteshvara, the bodhisattva of compassion, in response to the suffering of beings.
12 That is, with the thumb holding the tip of the ring finger down on the palm and the forefinger, middle finger, and little finger extended straight.
13 That is, with the hand held palm outward, fingers pointing up.
14 All of these are Buddhist masters devoted to the meditation practices of Tara.
15 Not identified; presumably some region in Asia.
16 Avalokiteshvara, Tara, and Padmasambhava.
17 That is, moving into a decline like the sun setting into the ocean.
18 A collective term for forces that work against the happiness

and welfare of beings and the flourishing of the Buddhist teachings.

19 The sign of the wheel of the dharma on the soles and palms is one of the thirty-two major marks of physical perfection gracing a buddha's form.

20 The Sanskrit form of the name Dawa Drolma (Tara of the Moon).

21 See Chapter 2, note 1.

22 Degeneration due to decreasing life span, increasing afflictive emotions, increasing resistance to spiritual teachings, increasing strife and conflict, and perversion of spiritual views.

23 That is, rebirth in the human realm seen as the ideal support or basis for achieving spiritual liberation.

24 This line seems corrupt in the manuscript and has been amended according to Chagdud Rinpoche's suggestions. Rinpoche felt that a possible version of the text might read, "If you are confused about cause and effect, you will endure unceasing suffering."

25 In Vajrayana Buddhism, the more elaborate rituals that empower a practitioner to train in specific meditation techniques involve four levels of empowerment.

26 See *The Hundred Thousand Songs of Milarepa*, Garma C. C. Chang, trans. (Boulder: Shambhala, 1977), vol. 2, pp. 357–361, "Tseringma and the Mudra Practice," for details of this encounter between Milarepa and the goddess Tseringma. The reference to the central channel relates to advanced yogic practices in Vajrayana Buddhism.

27 That is, Dawa Drolma's uncle, Drimed Khakyod Wangpo; see Chapter 1.

28 A karmic vision is a state of perception imposed on ordinary beings by their karma.

29 This individual, also mentioned in Chapter 1, was actually the incarnation of Dawa Drolma's maternal uncle, not her blood relation. It was Tromge Trungpa who prophesied to Chagdud

Rinpoche that his (Chagdud's) principal meditation practice would be that of Tara. Tromge Trungpa died when Chagdud Rinpoche was twenty-three, that is, in 1953 or 1954.

30 See Chapter 1, note 44.

5. The Staircase to Liberation

1 This is a reference to Padmasambhava, whose miraculous birth from a lotus is commemorated in the Seven-Line Supplication. See Chapter 1, note 2.

2 This stanza is a well-known prayer of praise to Avalokiteshvara, the bodhisattva embodying the compassion of all buddhas. The second line refers to the buddha Amitabha, lord of the lotus family; Avalokiteshvara is often depicted with Amitabha resting above the crown of his head.

3 As a feminine deity, Tara epitomizes the principle of emptiness as the fundamental nature of all phenomena. Emptiness can be thought of as both the "source" of all buddhas (since buddhahood is attained with the full realization of emptiness) and the field within which the qualities revealed by that realization unfold.

4 Ten 12-hour periods of day or night—in other words, five full days.

5 "The king and his subjects" refers to a group of twenty-five Tibetans who became intimate students of Padmasambhava during his sojourn in Tibet. This group comprises the king of Tibet, T'hrisrong Detzan, during whose reign Padmasambhava came to Tibet, and others (who, as Tibetans, were of course subjects of the king), including his queen, Yeshe Tsogyal, government ministers, and lay and ordained Buddhist masters.

6 That is, gathering merit, purifying the effects of harmful actions, and increasing one's positive qualities.

7 One of the eight major bodhisattvas, whose meditation is especially effective in purifying the effects of harmful actions that lead to rebirth in lower realms.

8 The awareness of all form as the form of the deity, all sound as mantra, and all thought and mental activity as the display of pristine awareness.

9 Body, speech, and mind.

10 See Chapter 2, note 67.

11 See Chapter 1, note 103.

12 See Chapter 3, note 10.